Charles Armand Miller

The way of the cross

A series of meditations on the history of our Lord

Charles Armand Miller

The way of the cross
A series of meditations on the history of our Lord

ISBN/EAN: 9783337257552

Printed in Europe, USA, Canada, Australia, Japan

Cover: Foto ©Lupo / pixelio.de

More available books at **www.hansebooks.com**

The Way of the Cross

A Series of Meditations
on the
History of the Passion of Our Lord

BY THE
Reverend C. Armand Miller, M.A.
Pastor of the Evangelical Lutheran Church of the Holy Trinity,
New York

NEW YORK   CHICAGO   TORONTO
Fleming H. Revell Company
Publishers of Evangelical Literature

TO MY TRUE HELPMEET,

In Loving Recognition

OF HER

Sympathy and Aid,

This Book

IS

Gratefully Inscribed.

PREFACE

SEVERAL inquiries, made at the beginning of the last Lenten season for a devotional book, arranged for daily use during the time of the memorial of our Lord's Passion, led to the surprising discovery that in the English language no such book exists. The writer thus had forced upon him the recognition of the need of a book which should contain, in simple, practical form, a daily Scripture lesson, and a plain, devotional exposition of its directly helpful and edifying teachings. The excellent works on Lenten themes that we now have, are not arranged for such systematic use, covering every day of Lent, nor do they lend themselves to the private devotions of the lay member of the Church who earnestly desires to make the holiest use of the sacred season, to his soul's highest profit. This little work seeks to supply the lack referred to. Its plan is very simple. It is based upon the division of the Passion History which may be found in the *Allgemeines Gebet-buch* of the General Lutheran Conference, (Leipzig, 1884) published under the special editorial supervision of Doctors Luthardt and Kliefoth. As that book, however, assigns

Preface

its first portion to the Monday after Invocavit Sunday, several meditations on the nature and true observance of Lent have here been prefixed, for the days from Ash Wednesday to Invocavit Sunday. The method of treatment is simple and obvious. Each Scripture lesson is followed by a study which seeks to direct earnest and prayerful attention to two objects: first, our Lord Himself, as shown in the passage considered; and secondly, the lessons for our own lives, found in that passage. Then follows a short prayer, in which the thoughts already noticed are concentered, and turned into praise and petition.

Edification has been the chief aim. But it is not claimed that even from this standpoint, the treatment embraces all of the practical themes that might have been drawn from the Scripture lessons. Careful attention has been given to the exegesis underlying the portions of Scripture treated, and it is believed that no position taken is devoid of good authority.

That God our Father may give His Holy Spirit to quicken and enforce the truth of His Word, so as to exalt and endear, to those who use this little book, His Son, our Lord Jesus Christ, in His passion,—this is the deepest prayer of him who sends it forth.

12th Sunday after Trinity, 1897.

Contents

	PAGE
Ash Wednesday	9
Thursday after Ash Wednesday	12
Friday after Ash Wednesday	16
Saturday after Ash Wednesday	20
Monday after Invocavit, which is the First Sunday in Lent	25
Tuesday after Invocavit	30
Wednesday after Invocavit	35
Thursday after Invocavit	40
Friday after Invocavit	46
Saturday after Invocavit	51
Monday after Reminiscere, which is the Second Sunday in Lent	56
Tuesday after Reminiscere	62
Wednesday after Reminiscere	68
Thursday after Reminiscere	73
Friday after Reminiscere	79
Saturday after Reminiscere	85
Monday after Oculi, which is the Third Sunday in Lent	92
Tuesday after Oculi	97
Wednesday after Oculi	103
Thursday after Oculi	109
Friday after Oculi	114
Saturday after Oculi	119
Monday after Laetare, which is the Fourth Sunday in Lent	125
Tuesday after Laetare	129
Wednesday after Laetare	136
Thursday after Laetare	142
Friday after Laetare	148

Contents

	PAGE
Saturday after Laetare	153
Monday after Judica, which is the Fifth Sunday in Lent	158
Tuesday after Judica	164
Wednesday after Judica	169
Thursday after Judica	173
Friday after Judica	178
Saturday after Judica	185
Monday after Palmarum, which is the Sixth Sunday in Lent	191
Tuesday after Palmarum	198
Wednesday after Palmarum	204
Thursday after Palmarum	209
Good Friday	215
Saturday after Palmarum	222

The Way of the Cross

Ash Wednesday

SCRIPTURE LESSONS: Joel 2: 12–19. Matt. 6: 16–21.

READ carefully, in the spirit of prayer, the two lessons. Then ponder; and apply by earnest heart-searching, to your own life, the meditation which follows.

Most appropriately has the Church appointed for this day, at the beginning of Lent, these lessons. They teach, distinctly enough, the meaning of this season of repentance and self-mortification upon which we have entered. The great principles that underlie our observance of the Church's great fast are here set before us, so that no one need mistake the nature or the purpose of this portion of the Church Year.

The prophet was commissioned to call *a solemn public fast*. The sin of the people made it necessary. Sin had brought judgment, and judgment was God's call to repentance. The Church, to-day also, has many reasons to recognize God's call to repentance. The living for self that is so common; the homes filled with every comfort and even luxury, while the work of the Lord languishes, and His servants suffer lack,—surely this is call for humiliation and turning. There is always need for individual repentance and renewal, but there is need also of solemn, public seasons of authorized appointment, to impress more deeply upon all the people the claims God has upon them, and their duty to acknowledge and respond to those claims. So, at this time, the word goes forth, Sanctify a fast; Gather the people; Let the ministers of the Lord weep and say, "Spare thy people, O Lord;" and Let the people turn unto the Lord their God. This is the first obvious meaning of the season of Lent.

This fast is to be *a heartfelt spiritual solemnity.* Clear is the warning. God wants rent hearts, not rent garments; the sincere hunger of the soul, not abstinence from meats and drinks, without the mourning of the heart over sin. He calls for self-denial and self-discipline in the sight of God, not assumed before men. The soul must get into the secret place with the Father, and bear His scrutiny. If, for the better mastery of the body, in order to keep it under, and to leave the soul the freer for spiritual contemplation and devotion, you abstain from food, let that be a secret between you and God. This is not a matter of rules and indulgences, least of all a matter of merit, but of heart-searching and of spiritual renewal in the sight of the Father who seeth in secret.

This fast means deep, true recognition of sin; sincere and whole-hearted turning unto God; prayer and communion with Him, secret and intense supplication to Him; fixing the heart on the heavenly treasures that are eternal and incorruptible; other-worldliness, instead of worldliness,—a heaven-fixed heart instead of a heart earth-bound. How easy it would be simply to have fish instead of meat, to rest from worldly dissipations for six weeks,—in order to gain more relish for them afterward,—and to count this the keeping of the fast! But God will not have it so. The spiritual fast He will have, or nothing. Are you ready to obey Him? He commands. Hear Him, and "turn with all your heart."

Prayer. Father in Heaven, search me and know my heart, try me and know my ways, and see if there be any wicked way in me, and lead me in the way everlasting. Spare me, O Lord, and pity me. Create in me a clean heart, and renew a constant spirit within me. Fix my heart where all true joys dwell, and let me be well-pleasing in Thy sight. See, Lord, I yield myself to Thee, that Thou mayest work Thy will with me, through thy gracious Spirit. And I ask for Jesus' sake. *Amen.*

Thursday after Ash Wednesday

Read Ex. 12 : 21–27; Heb. 10 : 19–31.

THE reason for the observance of Lent is *not legal*, but, like other evangelical rites and usages, is to be found in the free promptings of the cultivated Christian conscience and judgment. To appoint a memorial of noteworthy events has always been a natural human impulse. And to have set times for certain Christian duties, for certain public occasions of general interest, devoted to common supplication or humiliation, has always been recognized as fitting and profitable. On the basis of these two universally accepted ideas, uniting most fitly in this custom of the Church, the season of Lent finds not only justification, but authority. The sufferings of the Lord Jesus Christ, as the ground and means of the forgiveness of our sins, undoubtedly deserve especial memorial and commemoration. The sense of sin, and the contemplation of its awfulness (brought to the minds of men in no way so impressively as through the passion of our Lord), is of such universal import, and of such unceasing necessity, that the appropriateness of a stated, regularly recurring time for suitable meditations can scarcely be questioned.

It is certain that this feeling found expression very early in the ancient Church. Wednesday and Friday of every week were observed in remembrance of the sufferings of Christ, as days of humiliation and repentance. The development of the Church Year led to another manifestation of this same spirit in the observance of the Easter season. So deep was the effect of the commemoration of Christ's sufferings that one day, that of His death, was felt to be entirely too little time to devote to such a theme. By and by, therefore, Good Friday came to be preceded by a period set for prayer, repentance and fasting. This period finally was fixed as of forty days duration, with reference to the time our Master had consecrated by His fasting in the wilderness. The real significance of the Lenten observance can be profitably noted from the words of Chrysostom: "Many were heretofore used to come to the communion indevoutly and inconsiderately, especially at that time when Christ first gave it to His disciples. [In Holy Week.] Therefore our forefathers, considering the mischief arising from such careless approaches, met and appointed forty days for fasting and prayer, for hearing of sermons, and for holy assemblies; that all men in these days, being carefully purified by prayer and alms-deeds, fasting and watching, tears and confession of sins, with other like exercises, might, according to their capacity, come with pure consciences to the Holy Table."

That *set memorials are pleasing to God*, is evident from many teachings of His Word, as from the institution of the Passover, and of the holy Sacraments. Frequently also He, Himself, appointed times for public fasting and humiliation, of which one example is given in the lesson from the prophet Joel, so appropriately allotted to the first day of the Lenten season.

As we enter, then, this time of commemoration and repentance, we do it with the knowledge that the Church of old, by example and by precept, consecrated the keeping of the fast; that the principles which authorize it are clearly and repeatedly set forth in the Word of God; that it has been, in all the ages of the Christian Church, a time of especial devotion and spiritual refreshment; that it offers to each of us the opportunity for similar profit, and may, by a proper observance, become richly productive of good; that it is for the greater honor of our Lord, in the remembrance of His love and suffering, but still more in the exaltation of the atoning efficacy of His blood, and in moving to new contrition and holier living, those who bear His Name. Shall we not, then, embrace most gladly the privileges and blessings of the season, and rejoice in this call to turn from the ordinary course of life and give more of our thought and time and love to the things of Christ and of His kingdom?

Prayer. Dear Lord, make me love to think of Thee, of all that Thou hast done, of all that Thou hast been, and art to me. I thank Thee for having led Thy Church to fix this time to be a reminder of Thy passion, and a resting time, in sweet communion with Thee, from the weariness of pilgrimage. Be with me in my waiting. Give me fellowship with Thee and with the Father. And may this Lenten time be a true spiritual fast, and may my soul thereby grow strong. Through this holy usage, bind me in the bond of oneness with the Church of all ages, in the communion of saints. And grant my prayer acceptance, O Thou great High Priest, through the blood Thyself hast shed. *Amen.*

Friday after Ash Wednesday

Read again Matt. 6: 16-21.

THE true observance of Lent, as the lesson shows, is *not in externals*, but within. We are not to be desirous to have upon us the signs of extraordinary sacrifices, so that everyone who sees us will be aware of our piety. We are rather to take due pains to conceal the evidences of actual fasting or other self-deprivation, seeking the approval of the Father alone. It is an awful thing to have received one's reward, when it is such a poor and swiftly passing one. The hypocrite has an unenviable lot; he gets his reward, and has nothing beyond it. When he shall look for more at the last, he will find that he has already been fully repaid, in the praise of men, for the utterly worthless, though specious, pretence of piety that he wore as an outer garment. God has nothing to give him, for he did nothing, in the sight of God, to be approved. He wrought for the praise of men. He has his reward. But the thought and aim of the true Christian, in his keeping of the fast, is utterly different. He seeks only the Father's smile. How he appears before his Father, who sees in secret, is the only question to him. In other words, the true and worthy observance of Lent, is in the keeping of it as more than a cessation from some outward usages, more even than compliance with ecclesiastical customs, but as a spiritual and deeply religious concern. It is a thing of the heart. It is a close and intimate communion with God. Its rewards are of the inner, higher life, and, in their consummation, of the future life. Whoever will keep Lent otherwise is astray, and either deceived or seeking to deceive. This is the nature of the fast to which the Church and the Lord invite us. There is no other way to accept the invitation.

Yet *there is reward*, yes, treasure to be gained. It is not earthly, nor corruptible. This is a time especially for turning away from the earthly pursuits that tempt us, so strongly, to engross ourselves in them; and for thinking of the heavenly things and addressing ourselves with peculiar energy and concentration to the gaining of the heavenly treasures. Lent is a call to the loftier aspirations, a demand that we remember our celestial citizenship, and our eternal inheritance. We can afford, with profit, in every sense of the word, to relax the hitherto almost unceasing grind and toil, and to give more time to the assembling of ourselves together, more time to the Word of God, more time to prayer. There are some whose custom it is to read the Book of Books only on Sunday. Make your Lent one longer Sunday. If you had treasure in another land, you would love to read about it, to know perfectly the conditions on which you could lay claim to it, to talk with those who knew of it, and especially with any one able to be very helpful in securing the enjoyment of it. And so the themes of God's Word, the dwelling upon them in thought, the communion with Him in prayer,— these are the employments which, in unusual measure, ought to concern us during Lent. The very arrangement of this little book is intended to be helpful in showing a profitable way to use the Word of God: first, by giving careful attention to the words of the Scripture lesson; then by dwelling upon the passage as a whole, or verse by verse, and tasting its meaning, meditating upon it, and finding it yield up more and more of comfort and instruction; and then, by turning it into prayer, pleading the promises, deprecating the judgments, aspiring toward the glorious hopes, accepting the commands, and answering God's Word, with loving, loyal response. Thus prayer, on the basis of the Word, becomes what it ought to be, not monologue, but dialogue.

Give yourself to these things, now, in this peculiarly appropriate season. Learn the beauty and blessing of the Scriptures, as they reveal themselves only to a searcher of the

Book, and your deeper spiritual life will continue to develop, after the forty days are past.

Prayer. Lord, lift my heart toward the higher things. Let the heavenward trend possess my life with power. I am weary. Rest Thou me in the serene atmosphere which those breathe who live in the peace of God. Give me hunger for Thee, and for Thy Word. Give me joy in communing with Thee. I would be rich, but seeking after the treasures of this world, I have become poor; give me treasures in Heaven. Search me and try me by the life of Jesus, and deal with me in Thy secret places, that I may fast acceptably to Thee. Heal me in the inward parts, that I may please Thee. Grant all for the sake of Him who purchased for me a right to the life in Thee. *Amen.*

Saturday after Ash Wednesday

Read Isaiah 58: 1–12; Phil. 1: 3–11.

A TRUE inner quickening of the Christ-life will manifest itself, inevitably, in an *increase of good fruits* in the outer life. The connection is so intimate and necessary, that the prophet, in the first passage noted above, describes the fast as consisting of practical, loving deeds. Repentance is an intensely practical thing. "Bowing the head as a bulrush," and "spreading sackcloth and ashes" is not fasting, in a way acceptable to the Lord. "Loosing bands of wickedness, undoing heavy burdens, breaking yokes, dealing bread to the hungry," this is the fast that He has chosen. Repentance is not weeping over sin, while continuing to practice it; but renouncing sin, and undoing it. He does not truly repent who attends Lenten services, and loudly joins in the deprecations of the Litany, while he retains in his coffers the gains of unrighteousness and will not make restitution. Let your fast be in holy deeds, and in loving service.

Make this Lenten season *a time of self-denial*. "If any man will come after me, let him deny himself, and take up his cross daily, and follow me." Wherein does your Christian living involve self-denial? What cross,—that is, what voluntary burden or sacrifice, do you daily bear? Judged by this test of following, can you say that you are following Jesus at all? Is not this the very point at which the comfortable, ease-loving religion that is fashionable to-day, shows most unlikeness to the Christianity of Christ? What better purpose can we bring to the true observance of Lent than that of making it a school of self-sacrifice and cross-bearing, while we follow *Him*, in the carrying of *His* cross? Let this be, then, a time for thoughtful study of the appeals that Christ, in His Church, is making for your help, in the very pressing demands of the work which is yours, because it is His. Look around you, and where you see the need, either in your own congregation, or in the broader work of the Church, for your serving or your giving, heed the call and make response, even to the point of self-denial. Is it right to offer Him of that which costs you nothing? Did He offer you such a gift as that? If, under the dimmer light of the older day, King David would not accept the liberal gift of Araunah for a burnt offering, (2 Sam. 24: 18–25) but insisted upon paying him the full price of his land and oxen,—feeling unwilling to let another give and sacrifice for him,—then how much more should we, in our greater privileges and knowledge, refuse to depute our giving to another, or to content ourselves with offering God that which involves no sacrifice to us! Time, talent, service, money, whatever we have of which the Lord has need, and which He is willing to use, let us lay it freely upon His altar and rejoice that we are counted worthy to consecrate our gifts to Him!

Make your observance of this Lent the means of *a permanent uplifting of your spiritual life.* As St. Paul has it in the second lesson indicated above, " Abound yet more and more." To live nearer to Christ through these forty days, and then to turn your back upon Him, and give yourself to unrestrained worldliness in the marts, or in the drawing-rooms, for the months until the passion season comes again—this is no true keeping of the fast. Indeed, the keeping of it with this purpose and in this expectation, would be no better than hypocrisy. To repent for six weeks, is not to repent at all. A holiness that is intended to last for forty days, is a holiness of which the Lord knows nothing. The only vows He honors and approves, are eternal vows. The only renunciation of sin that avails before Him, is to renounce it forever. He will have no truce with sin, no armistice for the most part of the life, with a show of fighting for just the little time that we call Lent. If you are going back to the enemy's camp, you had as well stay there. Our Captain will never acknowledge you as soldier of His, unless you are His entirely. But this time of close inter-communion with Him is of inestimable benefit to every one who desires to be stronger and better for all the coming days. To be truly abiding with Him, even for a little while, will teach us the blessedness of such nearness, so that we should be lonely afterwards without Him. We draw nearer that we may never again go so far away. The lessons that we learn, will fit us to be far more to Him, and to do far more for Him, because we have been with Jesus. No wonder that others find no beauty nor worth in the observance of Lent, when they see men turn back, after the Easter feast, to the same empty life as before, and when they imagine that this is the keeping of the fast that the Church chooses, and that we suppose is pleasing to God. If all the future life is not better, nobler, fuller of praise and service, we have not kept the fast.

Prayer. O Lord, our Teacher and our Friend, help us that we may learn to know Thee as Thou art. If we may see Thy love, assuredly we shall love Thee! If we but know Thy Name, we cannot withhold our trust from Thee. If we have fellowship with Thy sorrows, we cannot forget Thee. Take us apart with Thee, as Thou didst take John and James and Peter, and show us Thyself in Thy moments of heart-revealing. Give us, for ourselves, the ambition of Paul for his spiritual children, to abound yet more and more. Make us unselfish, and teach us the privilege and the joy of sacrifice. Near to Thee, and in the shadow of Thine awful sufferings, surely shall we feel the hatefulness of sin, and abhor it; surely shall we feel the littleness of our lives, and commit ourselves to Thee for more abundant life. O Lord, Who seest our need, and Who hast died to save us from all unworthy things to all that is highest and best, supply our lack, and bless us in Thy love. *Amen.*

Monday after Invocavit, which is the First Sunday in Lent

Jesus therefore six days before the passover came to Bethany, where Lazarus was, whom Jesus raised from the dead. There they made him a supper in the house of Simon the leper; and Martha served: but Lazarus was one of them that sat at meat with him. And as he sat at meat there came a woman having an alabaster cruse of exceeding precious ointment, and she poured it upon his head and anointed the feet of Jesus, and wiped his feet with her hair: and the house was filled with the odor of the ointment. Judas Iscariot, one of his disciples, who should betray him, saith, Why was not this ointment sold for three hundred shillings and given to the poor? Now this he said, not because he cared for the poor; but because he was a thief, and having the bag took away what was put therein.

But there were some that had indignation among themselves, *saying*, To what purpose hath this waste of the ointment been made? For this ointment might have been sold for above three hundred shillings, and given to the poor. And they murmured against her.

But Jesus said, Let her alone; why trouble ye her? She hath wrought a good work on me. For ye have the poor always with you, and whensoever ye will ye can do them good: But me ye have not always. She hath done what she could: she hath anointed my body aforehand for the burying. And verily I say unto you, Wheresoever the gospel shall be preached throughout the whole world, that also which this woman hath done shall be spoken of for a memorial of her.

At a Feast. The Master is indeed at a festal scene. But He sees the shadow over Him. He catches the deeper, mysterious meaning of the loving deed of Mary. Before His instructed gaze there yawns, not far away, the open tomb, "For my burying she is come beforehand to anoint my body." What courage and consecration more than sublime are manifested in this fearless "forward march" into the jaws of death—the gates of hell. Not as in the shock and thrill of battle's glorious enthusiasm, but in the cool, calm, daily walk, He draws nearer each moment to the awful doom that the sin of others had prepared for Him.

And yet, as if this constant burden were not enough, we find Him here pained to the heart at the ignorant murmuring of some of the disciples, led by the deceitful indignation of Judas. Herein is a picture of the closing days of Jesus. Even though His friends are about Him—a feast prepared for Him—a man miraculously brought back from chains of death present as a living witness to His divine power,—yet He cannot avoid the clasp of sorrow. Grief's gaunt presence is inevitable;—and, "acquainted with grief," He feels now one thrust and now another, through His heart, of the swords that must pierce Him. And these sorrows that He bears are for you and me!

One Ray of Joy. Yet as we look at Him our hearts rejoice. Even though the days on which He is entering are to be so full of pain,—even though the traitor is now concocting his plans, —yet we have cause for joy to see Him once more in the house of His friends, Lazarus sitting with Him, Martha serving, and Mary pouring her richest gift on head and feet—the head that is so soon to bear the thorns, the feet that are to be pierced with the nail. One gleam of love-light in the midst of the gloom that blackens about Him. It makes the darkness darker still, but oh, how bright it seems by the contrast, and how tender the joy that it brought to the heart of the Master! What beauty of appropriateness He saw in it! What deathless reward He gave it!

1. Let us be moved, as we look on this scene, to *bring him our best*. What alabaster box have you? What offering very precious to the Saviour's heart does your love bid you bring? Have you broken the box of your heart's devotion, of your gifts of mind and body, of your ambitions and energies, upon His head? This was the best thing that Mary knew how to find and offer Him; she did "what she could." Have you offered Him your best? Is not now the fit time to do it? While foes were plotting and professed friends were finding fault, Mary stood up and honored Him. To-day, when so many hate Him and others mock His blessed Name, while half-hearted followers are plenty,

will you not put yourself without reserve at His disposal? Just now, at the beginning of this season of commemoration of His sufferings, does not every impulse of gratitude and loyalty drive *us* to love Him and to show our love unmistakably, in whatever way we can? Have you done what you could? Little or much, have you done it? *Will* you do what you can, the utmost that you can, for Him who, suffering and distressed and lonely, did all for you?

2. Let us be moved to abhor the *petty spirit of parsimony* of these disciples. Shall the heart of Jesus have no joy if it costs two hundred pence? Does *love* care for cost? Would God the Church to-day, you and I and all of us, had the heart of Mary! If she could have offered Him what cost her more, she would have done it. All true love is large and generous. The poor? Yes, we have them, and we owe them a sacred duty. But to Jesus we owe all. How blessed that we can give Him gladness even by succoring them. But are you afraid of giving *too much* to Christ? Are you one of those who ask, "Isn't this enough?" instead of asking, "Is this the very most that I can give?" The consummation of the plan of Christ and of the work of the Church will be wrought by the hands of those who have caught the noblest ambition of all, to do their utmost

for the glory of the King; not to limit their service by the least that the law demands, but to live to please God in the largest usefulness.

Prayer. O blessed Lord, Who didst bear for me the burdens that oppressed Thee, grant me Thy grace and power to render Thee my heart's deep gratitude. I have no alabaster box, no offering very precious, but, Lord, although my best is all unworthy to be given, I offer all my love, and all my strength, and all my hopes and all I am and can be by Thy grace, to Thee forever. Take Thou, and seal and keep the gift, O Thou Who gavest all for me. *Amen.*

Tuesday after Invocavit

On the morrow a great multitude that had come unto the feast, when they heard that Jesus was coming to Jerusalem, took the branches of the palm trees, and went forth to meet him, and cried out, Hosanna: Blessed *is* he that cometh in the name of the Lord, even the King of Israel. And Jesus, having found a young ass, sat thereon; as it is written, Fear not, daughter of Zion: behold, thy King cometh, sitting on an ass's colt.

The multitude therefore that was with him when he called Lazarus out of the tomb, and raised him from the dead, bare witness. For this cause also the multitude went and met him, for that they heard that he had done this sign. The Pharisees therefore said among themselves, Behold how ye prevail nothing: lo, the world is gone after him.

Now the feast of unleavened bread drew nigh which is called the passover. And Jesus said to his disciples, Ye know that after two days the passover cometh, and the Son of man is delivered up to be crucified. Then were gathered together the chief priests, and the elders of the people, unto the court of the high priest, who was called Caiaphas; and they took counsel together that they might take Jesus by subtilty, and kill him. But they said, Not during the feast, lest a tumult arise among the people.

Then one of the twelve, who was called Judas Iscariot, went away, and communed with the chief priests and captains, and said, What are ye willing to give me, and I will deliver him unto you? And they were glad, and covenanted to give him money; and they weighed unto him thirty pieces of silver. And he consented, and sought opportunity to deliver him unto them without tumult.

The Master Honored. Our Lord comes before

us here unlike Himself. It is His first and last acceptance (in the time of His humiliation) of human honor. Rang the "Hosannas" sweetly in His ear, or heard He, like their echo, the cry "Crucify Him! Crucify Him!"? Here He is coming as a King. Oh, lowly King! A passing wave of popular enthusiasm had lifted Him up before this multitude. All about Him now are praises, honors! His enemies, not shrewd enough to understand, lose courage. "Ye behold how ye accomplish nothing. All the world is gone after Him."

But Not Deceived. No momentary enthusiasm has deceived the Master. The deep pain that cannot pass is gnawing at His heart. He weeps at the certain doom of the people, about to reject Him. He foresees every part of the evil that is to come. Calmly He said it, and carelessly His disciples seem to have heard it, yet who can realize what horror was in his human heart when He spoke the words, "The Son of man will be delivered up to be crucified;" as He looked the while down into the coming days, to those last, long hours, fearful in hatred, lurid with the wrath of His foes, cruel in the agony they should bring, red with the blood of His heart. Even now as He speaks, the foes are gathered, taking counsel, not for the justice or right to defend which they were set, but how, by craft, they may take and kill Him. Even now the traitor is stealing forth on His hellish errand to the cowardly enemies that thirst only for the blood of the Lord, that he may barter for base gain the Master who had called and taught and loved him.

And serene in His sorrow and danger, the Saviour walks steadfastly the path appointed Him, whose end He sees. *For you;* for if He had faltered and failed, your sin had sealed your awful fate forever.

1. Let us not leave our *enthusiasm unrooted.* Enthusiasm is good, but if it has no depth it avails nothing. The mob howls to-day for the blood of its hero of yesterday. See the story of the French Revolution for illustrations abundant. Emotions are easily stirred, and it is no great distance from the men of Jerusalem, with their "Hosannas" of Palm Sunday and their "Crucify Him" of Good Friday, to those who, to-day, weep at the sufferings of Jesus during Lent, and put Him to an open shame the day after Easter. Yet if enthusism be grounded in the intelligent devotion of the will to the Lord, it becomes the fervent zeal of a Paul and a Luther.

2. Fail not to remember that *no man comes into contact with Jesus and remains neutral.* Christ, and especially Christ in His passion,

divides men. Here are the shouting multitude and the docile disciples, but here are also the murmuring Pharisees, the plotting Sanhedrin, the crouching, subtle, greedy traitor! Every man, when Christ comes into the horizon of his life, is either for Him or against Him. Where are you? Force the question on your heart insistently. Not, where are you counted by your fellow-men; not, where do you profess to be,—but *where are you?* When Christ is opposed and betrayed, are you, for good and ill, for time and for eternity,—are you on His side?

3. *Learn how subtle is the approach of sin.* Covetousness, avarice, the desire of gain grown masterful, what may it not work? Poor Judas never thought when he first found the carrying of the bag so pleasant, that he would become a thief, and then the seller of the Saviour. Nay, when he had gone so far as to strike this shameful bargain, he little thought it meant the blood and death of Jesus. Sin never shows its "horrid front" in all its ugliness, when first it woos its timid victim. Do you fear its first and lightest invitation? Do you distrust and flee its slightest approach? God give you to be afraid!

Prayer. O Saviour Who hast suffered, and hast not halted though the end was plain before Thee, grant that my heart, in steadfast and unchanging adoration, may praise Thee with "Hosannas." Though all else should strive against Thee, give me in loyal, loving faith to claim Thee as King. Since I am so weak, O strengthen me, that neither dread of danger, greed of gain, nor any other hostile power may serve to turn me from my Lord, Who loved me and gave Himself for me. *Amen.*

Wednesday after Invocavit

And on the first day of unleavened bread, when they sacrificed the passover, his disciples say unto him, Where wilt thou that we go and make ready that thou mayest eat the passover?

And he sent Peter and John, and said unto them, Behold, when ye are entered into the city, there shall meet you a man bearing a pitcher of water; follow him into the house whereinto he goeth. And ye shall say unto the goodman of the house, The Master saith unto thee, My time is at hand. Where is the guest-chamber, where I shall eat the passover with my disciples? And he will himself shew you a large upper room furnished: there make ready. And they went, and found as he had said unto them: and they made ready the passover.

And when it was evening, and the hour was come, he sat down, and the apostles with him. And he said unto them, With desire I have desired to eat this passover with you before I suffer: for I say unto you, I shall not eat it, until it be fulfilled in the kingdom of God. And he received a cup, and when he had given thanks, he said, Take this, and divide it among yourselves: for I say unto you, I shall not drink from henceforth of the fruit of the vine, until the kingdom of God shall come.

And there arose also a contention among them, which of them was accounted to be greatest. And he said unto them, The kings of the Gentiles have lordship over them; and they that have authority over them are called Benefactors. But ye *shall* not *be* so: but he that is the greater among you, let him become as the younger; and he that is chief, as he that doth serve. For whether is greater, he that sitteth at meat, or he that serveth? is not he that sitteth at meat? but I am in the midst of you as he that serveth. But ye are they that have continued with me in my trials; and I appoint unto you a kingdom, even as my Father appointed unto me, that ye may eat and drink at my table in my kingdom; and ye shall sit on thrones judging the twelve tribes of Israel.

Preparing for the Sacrifice. The gentle, loving, pathetic figure of the Master assumes new interest. The hour draws nearer, and He takes guidance of those preparations which must have seemed like the building of the scaffold by the victim. Not blessed, like Isaac, with the ignorance that could ask "where is the lamb for the offering?" He, knowing Himself to be the sacrifice, selected with firm and unhesitating spirit, the place where the passover should be eaten and the last hours spent. Not for an instant has He forgotten all that it means. "Tell the householder," says He, "my time is at hand."

Around the Board. It is the hour of evening. His full heart yearns over these, His friends. He gives most loving expression of His longing for this hour of fellowship with them—this blessed communion around the passover board—this time when, in the mysterious spiritual exaltation of the hour, they could better receive and appreciate some of the precious and sacred truths for which they had never yet been fit. It was to be a heart-to-heart communion, and His soul longed to refresh itself in this loving service before He should go out to gloom and agony. Yet sadness lingered, in spite of the realization of His longing. The approaching separation throws its shadow upon Him. "I will not drink henceforth of the fruit of the vine until that day when I drink it new with you in my Father's kingdom."

A new grief comes to His already sorely burdened heart. All His teaching, and all His example have not sufficed to give spiritual insight and sympathy to these dull disciples. Not realizing what He says, they are quarreling about the official station each is to have in that Kingdom which, so they fatuously dream, He is about to establish. "A strife among them" in this hour of all hours. The rudest sort of discord for His soul to hear, tuned as it was to high and tender themes. He was alone, as He had always been, and as we shall see Him again. Yet no rebuke is in His mouth; only loving teaching concerning the beauty of humility, and then wonderful promises of the rewards and blessings that are yet to be.

1. *Learn a lesson of trustful obedience.* Our hearts ought to rest in the proof we have here,—a proof hallowed by association with His passion,—of Jesus' provision for every need and of His direction, in all things, of His children. Wise were they in asking only Him, "Where wilt thou that we shall eat?" Let the Master arrange and provide. The where, and how, and

when, of our lives are His affair. He who could take thought like this, and notice even the pitcher belonging to the man whose heart and home would welcome them, will not fail to see the every need of every life submitted to His care, and take thought for *you*. Let there be only an obedient trust; and, as it was then, so will it always be "found as He said unto them." Be not afraid nor anxious.

2. *A Lesson of Fellowship.* Shall we not appreciate the love and friendship of our Lord? The intensity of His desire was not so fully met as it should have been. Shall His longing for closeness to us, for kinship and communion, have from us no response to that blessed fellowship He offers? We hear Him speak of His desire; and do not our hearts faint and sicken as we think how we have desired all other things more than His fellowship? Shall not we be ashamed and repentant, that He, the Altogether Lovely, should crave our love and tenderness, and yet be met and pierced with our indifference?

3. *A Lesson of Humility.* Who is great? God's thoughts are not our thoughts as we answer. Ask the world, Who is the greatest? and the last one to whom the world will point is the one that serves. Yet he is God's great man. What is your standard of greatness? Will you be ambitious? It is right to be ambitious;

only seek not any greatness save that which God counts great. Then you cannot be too ambitious. Which is more important, God's opinion or that of the heathen? Do you care to please self and the world, or Him?

4. *A Lesson of Faithfulness.* These men were poor, dull pupils in the school of grace, but to their utmost they were faithful. They *continued.* God give us the grace of continuance! Even in His trials and sorrows and the assaults of Satan, thus far they had continued. So let us continue with Him in His temptations. In this Lenten season let us continue in our thoughts, in our prayers, in our sympathy, in our service; let us continue in the fellowship of His suffering. There is rich reward. It is good to continue with Him through good and through ill report.

Prayer. O Lord of Love, Who guidest and carest for Thine own, help us to trust Thee and to dwell in Thine unchanging peace. Help us to long for Thee, even as the hart panteth for the water brooks; to find Thee, to taste of Thee, to drink the living water, never again to thirst! Deliver us from the deadness of indifference. Make us to abide in fellowship with Thee, and so deliver us from sin and death and hell, O Thou Who hast in bitterest strife, conquered these our deadly foes. *Amen.*

Thursday after Invocavit

Now before the feast of the passover, Jesus knowing that his hour was come that he should depart out of this world unto the Father, having loved his own who were in the world, he loved them unto the end. And during supper, the devil having already put into the heart of Judas Iscariot, Simon's *son*, to betray him, *Jesus,* knowing that the Father had given all things into his hands, and that he came forth from God, and goeth unto God, riseth from supper, and layeth aside his garments; and he took a towel, and girded himself. Then he poureth water into the bason, and began to wash the disciples' feet, and to wipe them with the towel wherewith he was girded. So he cometh to Simon Peter. He saith unto him, Lord, dost thou wash my feet? Jesus answered and said unto him, What I do thou knowest not now; but thou shalt understand hereafter. Peter saith unto him, Thou shalt never wash my feet. Jesus answered him, If I wash thee not, thou hast no part with me. Simon Peter saith unto him, Lord, not my feet only, but also my hands and my head. Jesus saith to him, He that is bathed needeth not save to wash his feet, but is clean every whit: and ye are clean, but not all. For he knew him that should betray him; therefore said he, ye are not all clean.

So when he had washed their feet, and taken his garments, and sat down again, he said unto them, Know ye what I have done to you? Ye call me Master, and, Lord: and ye say well; for so I am. If I then, the Lord and the Master, have washed your feet, ye also ought to wash one another's feet. For I have given you an example, that ye also should do as I have done to you. Verily, verily, I say unto you, A servant is not greater than his lord; neither one that is sent greater than he that sent him. If ye know these things, blessed are ye if ye do them. I speak not of you all: I know whom I have chosen: but that the scripture may be fulfilled, He that eateth my bread lifted up his heel against me. From henceforth I tell you before it come to pass, that, when it is come to pass, ye may believe that I am *he*. Verily, verily, I say unto you, He that receiveth whomsoever I send receiveth me; and he that receiveth me receiveth him that sent me.

Loving to the End. The pathetic meaning of the words, "He loved them to the end" we can never fathom. They are the key to the whole story of the life of Jesus, and most of all, appropriate to His passion. "Having loved His own, He loved them to the end," though He knew that His time was come. The time of His deepest humiliation, the time for His agonizing suffering, the time for the strange mystery of death for sinners, under the burden of their sin, the time for glorifying the name of the Father, as it never had been glorified, the time for the testing and showing forth of matchless love—when this time was come, and He knew it, He loved them to the end. This is more than human love. A mother's love has failed in agonies far less than these which He was entering upon, and in the desperation of the struggle for her life, she has forgotten the fruit of her own body, and given it to save herself,—but Jesus loved unto the end. At any cost, at every cost, His love won the victory; and, looking into the face of death, the lurid glare of hell, the abandonment by His Father, the appropriation of that weight of sin which would set Him apart as the outcast of the human race, He shrank not nor withdrew. This was love to the end. No wonder St. John, seeking through the universe for the great example, found none other than this, and called aloud, "Herein is love, that He loved us," "Hereby know we love, because He laid down His life for us." (1 John 4: 10; 3: 16.)

What He Knew. He could not have borne His intolerable burden, but for the strength that came to His soul with other knowledge. "Knowing that the Father had given all things into His hand, and that He came forth from God, and goeth unto God," cheered, nerved, and comforted by this knowledge, He could endure and persevere. He had laid aside the use of His Divine Powers, save where they were needed for His Father's glory and the accomplishment of His task; but in these last days of passion His Oneness with the Father in His Divine Nature, upheld and gave Him power which no mere man could have possessed.

The Servant of All. With this knowledge, in this strength, He rises and becomes their servant; doing most menial work for them, teaching these poor, unspiritual souls, by deeds, what He had just been telling them in words; He bears with impetuous ignorant Peter, and speaks calmly of the traitor, who having eaten His bread, now lifteth up his heel against Him. He is face to face with His awful agony and death, with no soul to sympathize, and with the traitor's falseness pressing on His heart. Thus we see Him, in this day's lesson. Oh, for hearts to feel His woe, endured for us.

1. *The devil dares even to enter the presence of Jesus.* Nearness to Christ does not defend us from Satan's assaults and power, unless we are spiritually near to Him. What had the adversary to do with this feast? Yet he was there; and to-day he is in the pulpit, in the pew, at the chancel rail, beside us in our prayers and Bible reading. Making the sign of the cross does not affright him. He who was at the feast will not fail to be at our holiest places in our holiest seasons. Only the heart that denies him, and cleaves, in living faith, to Christ the Saviour, is safe.

2. *Our hearts are prone to rely on their own wisdom, and not to submit to Christ.* Peter thought he was honoring Jesus, in saying, "Thou shalt never wash my feet," but he was dishonoring his Lord. He was assuming that he knew better than his Master, what was right and becoming. He was mistaken, but we make the same mistake. Beware of judgments and opinions after the flesh. Jesus knows, far bet-

ter than you and I, what is good for us. Oh, let Him have His way with you!

3. *Many problems find their solution* in that word of loving rebuke to Peter, "What I do, thou knowest not now, but thou shalt understand hereafter." We should feel in our perplexities about our Lord and His dealings with us, about our sorrows, trials and disappointments, that it is waste of time to ponder and wonder and seek to know *now!* We should find rest in the sure promise that we shall understand hereafter. "I can't understand why I should be so afflicted;"—we hear it almost every day. Poor, sore soul, you do not need to understand. You need only to trust *now*, to that love that loves on to the end. But be not discouraged. You *shall* understand! Wait only for His time. What mysteries and what comfort that "hereafter" holds within its secret heart.

4. *True humility is not for show nor for speech, but for service.* Christlike humility does not spend itself in idle protestations. It springs from Christlike love, and like all love, it labors. No servant was in the upper chamber, and each disciple was unwilling to do the menial office of washing the dusty, sandaled feet,—a customary courtesy. So Jesus did it, and we are to do it. Whenever, in the service of the Church or of our fellow-men, humble

help is needed, you and I are to be ready to give it. Are you proud? Too proud to take the lowly place of service that is offered you? "If I, your Lord and Master, have washed your feet" will you not minister, in lowliest service to My least ones?

5. *To call Him Lord and Master means obedience.* It means loyalty. It means going when He says, "Go"; and coming when He says, "Come"; and doing it, when He says, "Do this." It means unquestioning promptness to perform His bidding. You call Him Saviour. Have you known what it means to call Him Lord and Master?

Prayer. O Christ, Whose love has never failed, Whose kingliness was hidden in the form of a servant, I look to Thee, of Thy deep love, to shield me from my soul's great enemy; to make and keep me humble and obedient, resting in Thee amidst the trials of my life, seeking to serve Thee, in my service to Thy Church and to Thy brethren. I would withhold from Thee and from Thy governance, not one thing of all that Thou hast given me, for Thou hast not withheld Thyself from pain and death for me. Take me, and use and bless me, loving Lord. *Amen.*

Friday after Invocavit

When Jesus had thus said, he was troubled in spirit, and testified, and said, Verily, verily, I say unto you, that one of you shall betray me. Then the disciples looked one on another, doubting of whom he spake.

And as they sat and were eating, Jesus said, Verily I say unto you, One of you shall betray me, *even* he that eateth with me. They began to be sorrowful, and to say unto him one by one, Is it I ? And he said unto them, *It is* one of the twelve, he that dippeth with me in the dish.

Now there was leaning on Jesus' bosom one of his disciples, whom Jesus loved. Simon Peter therefore beckoned to him, that he should ask who it should be of whom he spake. He then lying on Jesus' breast saith unto him, Lord, who is it ? Jesus answered, He it is, to whom I shall give a sop, when I have dipped *it*. And when he had dipped the sop, he gave *it* to Judas Iscariot, *the son* of Simon.

And he said, The Son of man goeth, even as it is written of him : but woe unto that man through whom the Son of man is betrayed! good were it for that man if he had not been born. And Judas, which betrayed him, said, Is it I, Rabbi? He saith unto him, Thou hast said. And after the sop, then entered Satan into him. Jesus therefore saith unto him, That thou doest, do quickly. Now no man at the table knew for what intent he spake this unto him. For some thought, because Judas had the bag, that Jesus said unto him, Buy what things we have need of for the feast; or, that he should give something to the poor. He then having received the sop went out straightway: and it was night.

Therefore, when he was gone out, Jesus said, Now is the Son of man glorified, and God is glorified in him. If God be glorified in him, God shall also glorify him in himself, and shall straightway glorify him.

Deepening Gloom. Let us linger again with the Master. The scene is the same, but the opening words of the lesson tell us of the ever deepening gloom that was oppressing the heart of Jesus. "He was troubled in the spirit." "A wounded spirit, who can bear?" The time He had apprehended, when the blackness of treachery must be revealed, was at hand: the time to draw the line between honest and dishonest men, to separate between simple-hearted loyalty and the hypocritical traitor; the time that marked the actual beginning of the piercing of His heart. "He was troubled in the spirit."

A Warning Word. A heart that had no such love in it as Jesus' had, would not have felt this blow so keenly. If His love had not been more than any other love He could not have persevered. Even now He speaks, although too late to save the criminal from his deed of wretched sin and folly, a warning word: "The Son of man goeth as it is written of Him,"—(and none but He felt what that "going" meant)—"but woe unto that man through whom the Son of man is betrayed! Good were it for that man if he had not been born." But the traitor's ears are closed, his heart is seared. He has sold himself to Satan of his own free choice; and the Master at last sends him forth —away from the inner circle, away from the friends of Jesus. This "What thou doest do quickly," was the judgment of Judas. Then, and not when he had hanged himself, was his doom fixed. The Master felt that the hour must speed. Not much longer could He endure the polluting presence. And He had that to do and say which the traitor's presence made impossible. Yes, He who is love, out of love for those who love Him, has spoken and will speak again the word that shall send to the outer darkness His foes.

1. *How much sorrow sin brings!* If only the sinner suffered, sin would not be so terrible. But Jesus was troubled in spirit, and the disciples began to be sorrowful, and if the angels knew, they doubtless wept, all because of the crime of one traitor. Even those who did not understand what was transpiring felt a malign and distressful influence upon them. And the traitors to Jesus to-day,—those who, in His livery, assail Him by false teaching, lessening His influence, and tending to destroy His power; or those who bear His name, but lack His spirit, denying the power while they hold the form of godliness;—these, too, bring sorrow to Him who shall not be satisfied until He sees of the travail of His soul, and they bring sorrow to the Church and to the friends of Jesus. How horrible is treachery to Christ! Oh, the

awfulness of selling Jesus, by yielding conviction and truth, for gain or selfish satisfaction!

2. We can sympathize with those honest souls, who, although sure of their sincerity, were yet *distrustful of themselves*, and asked, Is it I, Lord; Is it possible that I am wounding Thee, or that I could betray Thy cause? O keep me, for I cannot be sure of myself, unless through every day and every hour, my life is hid with Thee in God! Let us be more diffident and suspicious of ourselves and of our capacity to resist sin! Far better ask with these honest but weak disciples, "Lord, is it I?" than sing, "Surely the Captain may depend on me!" Then, too, would that we were more ready to ask the question when He sends forth the cry for workers, ministers, missionaries, men to strengthen and sustain with consecrated gifts the work of the church! Who is His chosen one? "Lord, is it I?"

3. What *a blessed pillow* is the breast of Jesus! Oh, for more Johns who will lie there, whose hearts beat in sympathy with His, who with zeal and devotion, like the Beloved Disciple, find the fire of their souls renewed by abiding in closest communion with Him. John's life of activity is explained by the nearness of his spiritual communion with Jesus. We do not abide enough in fellowship with our Master, through prayer and the study

of His word, so that He may fill us with His Spirit and send us forth with shining faces to His work.

4. "*Glorified.*" Are you, too, ready to glorify God as Jesus did? The glory of obedience even unto the uttermost, is it the glory you are giving Him? The glory of self-sacrifice for Him and in His cause, do you know it? The glory that comes through patient endurance of the trials He sends, the sorrows that come from *His* hand, is this your sphere? Thus the beloved Son gave glory to His Father, and we too can give Him glory. (John 15: 8.)

Prayer. O Christ, whose heart was troubled by the treachery of Thy disciple, grant me a steadfast, faithful spirit of obedience and love; to the end that, heart to heart with Thee, my life may show Thy spirit, and may glorify Thy Name, whether in service or in sacrifice and sorrow. *Amen.*

Saturday after Invocavit

And as they were eating, Jesus took bread, and blessed, and brake it; and he gave to the disciples, and said, Take, eat; this is my body; this do in remembrance of me. And the cup, in like manner after supper, and gave thanks, and gave to them, saying, Drink ye all of it; for this is my blood of the covenant, which is shed for you and for many unto remission of sins. But I say unto you, I shall not drink henceforth of this fruit of the vine, until that day when I drink it new with you in my Father's kingdom. And they all drank of it.

Little children, yet a little while I am with you. Ye shall seek me: and as I said unto the Jews, Whither I go, ye cannot come; so now I say unto you. A new commandment I give unto you, that ye love one another; even as I have loved you, that ye also love one another. By this shall all men know that ye are my disciples, if ye have love one to another.

Simon Peter saith unto him, Lord, whither goest thou? Jesus answered, Whither I go, thou canst not follow me now; but thou shalt follow afterward. Peter saith unto him, Lord, why cannot I follow thee even now? I will lay down my life for thee. And in like manner also said they all. Jesus answereth, Wilt thou lay down thy life for me? Verily, verily, I say unto thee, the cock shall not crow, till thou hast denied me thrice.

Simon, Simon, behold, Satan asked to have you, that he might sift you as wheat: but I made supplication for thee, that thy faith fail not: and do thou, when once thou hast turned again, stablish thy brethren. And he said unto him, Lord, with thee I am ready to go both to prison and to death. And he said, I tell thee, Peter, the cock shall not crow this day, until thou shalt thrice deny that thou knowest me.

And he said unto them, When I sent you forth without purse, and wallet, and shoes, lacked ye anything? And they said, Nothing. And he said unto them, But now, he that hath a purse, let him take it, and likewise a wallet: and he that hath none, let him sell his cloke, and buy a sword. For I say unto you, that this which is written must be fulfilled in me, And he was reckoned with transgressors: for that which concerneth me hath fulfilment. And they said, Lord, behold, here are two swords. And he said unto them, It is enough.

Love's Feast. The Master is unwilling to leave His disciples, and to leave those who should afterward believe on Him through their word, without a tangible, visible remembrance of Him, a means of communion with Him, of partaking of Him. In these solemn hours of the last night, amidst associations and influences forever memorable, He breaks the bread that becomes the mystic means of sharing in His body, and gives the cup that brings to him who takes, the blood also of the New Testament. Forever holy, precious Sacrament,—how short of sight and hurtful to themselves are those who count it naught, or empty it of what our Lord put in it, at this most impressive institution of the Feast!

What a reminder of His love it is, not only in its very essence, but by recalling to us how, at this awful season, He was not thinking of Himself but of His dear disciples;—not of His sufferings, but of the church He was about to purchase with His blood, and which through this most refreshing and salutary feast, should show His death until He come!

Still Self-Forgetful. And now, still self-forgetful, tenderly He strengthens and prepares His loved ones for the tragic separation He foresees—" A little while," He says, and He tells them of strange trials about to encompass them, of the prayers that He is offering and of the terrible doom that hangs above Him. His burden was made heavier because they did not understand. He had no sympathy. The heart's deepest need, a friend who knows and feels, He had not. "Lord, here are two swords;" —so literal and earthly in their interpretation, were they, with no thought of the spirit of His words!

1. The meaning of the Holy Supper appears in view of *the circumstances of its institution.* If it had been commanded long afterward, through Peter or Paul, it could never have seemed what it is, even though it had brought the same grace to us. But now, when we approach the feast, we may always imagine that table in the upper room, the solemn faces of the eleven, the strange mingling of majesty and manhood in the Master,—and without, the form of the traitor slinking through the darkness, and just ahead, Gethsemane, the torches, the

trials, the scourge, the mob, the yells of rage, the cross! Oh, count, dear ransomed soul, the price of this feast, and stay not away when the table is spread! It cost too much for us to prize it lightly. Come, show your Saviour's death and look forward to His coming! Feed on this Bread of Heaven, drink of this Wine of Heaven, and be refreshed. God forbid that we should name His Name, and yet, despise the feast of His Body and Blood.

2. With tender power comes from the Lord of Love, in this supremest hour of sacrifice for love's sake, *the command to love each other*. What a measure His own love furnishes,—"As I have loved you,"—when we hear those words coming to us from out this agony of love's self-abnegation! *Thus* are we to love one another. And a marked manifestation of love is demanded when He tells us that our love is to be the badge of our discipleship. "By this shall all men know that ye are my disciples, because ye have love one toward another." Such was, indeed, the love of the early Christians. In plague and pestilence, in trial and persecution, the followers of the Nazarene so clung to one another that the heathen, astonished, could not but recognize a strange, new power in the world. It is not enough to feel love ; we must show it. All men should know us by our mutual love. Are you thus marked as a disciple of the Lov-

ing One? Think of this. Meditate and search your heart as to this duty, so tenderly and solemnly enjoined.

3. *The mystery of temptation and trial, how strange it is!* Why could not He who assured the final victory of Peter have prevented the temptation also? We do not know. It is enough that He wills it. But is it not suggestive that after this temptation and fall, Peter never again was self-confident? Some men can be taught no otherwise than by failure. Could this self-deceived, impetuous, untried Peter ever have strengthened his brethren as the chastened, instructed, rescued Peter did? Count upon it, God has a purpose in suffering us to be tried,—a purpose for ourselves, and for our influence. Have you been tried? Have you been preserved? Are you strengthening your brethren?

Prayer. Lord, Who knowest us in our weakness and our need; Who knowest our powers to suffer and endure; give us the training and the testing which Thou seest we ought to have, but keep us through it all! Burn out our dross and make us strong to love and thus to testify for Thee. And give us power to glorify Thy Name among our brethren, Thou Who hast so loved us. *Amen.*

Monday after Reminiscere, which is the second Sunday in Lent

Let not your heart be troubled: believe in God, believe also in me. In my Father's house are many mansions; if it were not so, I would have told you; for I go to prepare a place for you. And if I go and prepare a place for you, I come again, and will receive you unto myself; that where I am, *there* ye may be also. And whither I go, ye know the way. Thomas saith unto him, Lord, we know not whither thou goest; how know we the way? Jesus saith unto him, I am the way, and the truth, and the life: no one cometh unto the Father, but by me. If ye had known me, ye would have known my Father also: from henceforth ye know him, and have seen him. Philip saith unto him, Lord, shew us the Father, and it sufficeth us. Jesus saith unto him, Have I been so long time with you, and dost thou not know me, Philip? he that hath seen me hath seen the Father; how sayest thou, Shew us the Father? Believest thou not that I am in the Father, and the Father in me? the words that I say unto you I speak not from myself: but the Father abiding in me doeth his works. Believe me that I am in the Father, and the Father in me: or else believe me for the very works' sake. Verily, verily, I say unto you, He that believeth on me, the works that I do shall he do also; and greater *works* than these shall he do; because I go unto the Father. And whatsoever ye shall ask in my name, that will I do, that the Father may be glorified in the Son. If ye shall ask anything in my name, that will I do. If ye love me, ye will keep my commandments. And I will pray the Father, and he shall give you another Comforter, that he may be with you forever, *even* the Spirit of truth: whom the world cannot receive; for it beholdeth him not, neither knoweth him: **ye** know him; for he abideth with you, and shall be in you. I will not leave you desolate: I come unto you. Yet a little while, and the world beholdeth me no more; but ye behold me: because I live, ye shall live also. In that day ye shall know that I am in my Father, and ye in me, and I in you. He that hath my commandments, and keepeth them, he it is that loveth me: and he that loveth me shall be loved of my Father, and I will love him, and will manifest myself unto him. Judas (not Iscariot) saith unto him, Lord, what is come to pass that thou wilt manifest thyself unto us, and not unto the world? Jesus answered and said unto him, If a man love me, he will keep my word: and my Father will love him, and we will come unto him, and make our abode with him. He that loveth me not keepeth not my words: and the word which ye hear is not mine, but the Father's who sent me.

These things have I spoken unto you, while *yet* abiding with you. But the Comforter, *even* the Holy Spirit, whom the Father will send in my name, he shall teach you all things, and bring to your remembrance all that I said unto you. Peace I leave with you; my peace I give unto you: not as the world giveth, give I unto you. Let not your heart be troubled, neither let it be fearful. Ye heard how I said to you, I go away, and I come unto you. If ye loved me, ye would have rejoiced, because I go unto the Father: for the Father is greater than I. And now I have told you before it come to pass, that, when it is come to pass, ye may believe. I will no more speak much with you, for the prince of the world cometh: and he hath nothing in me; but that the world may know that I love the Father, and as the Father gave me commandment, even so I do. Arise, let us go hence.

Let not your heart be troubled. His own heart near the time when it would break with the weight of the world's sin, hear this wonderful lover of men say to His disciples, "Let not *your* heart be troubled." Bidding them trust in Him He tells them where He is going, and why,—then tells them to look again for His coming. Men count Him only the greatest of human heroes, but He did not so count Himself. Hear Him say, "I am the Way and the Truth and the Life." No other man ever dared utter such words as these. If He is not Very God of Very God, then the Jews were right, and we with them must take up stones to punish the blasphemer. But He *is* the Way, and that because He is the truth and the life. For only he who knows the truth as it is in Christ Jesus, and who shares the life of the Saviour (1 John 5: 12), is in the Way, and shall enter the blessed city which is the goal. To know the truth is not enough; one must live it. Pure doctrine, received and defended ever so ardently, is not truly appropriated unless it shows in the life. Christ is really mine, to save and bless me, only when my life, lived in His Spirit, enforces the truth that my faith concerning Him is correct in substance. To him to whom He is the Truth and the Life, Christ is also the Way.

The Message Concerning Himself. Here is the message of Christ about Himself, in the closing hours of His earthly life. He is the Way; He is one with the Father; He is the sender of the Holy Spirit; whoso honors the Father truly, honors Him in the Son; whoso receives the Holy Ghost, the Paraclete, receives Him as the gift of the Father and the Son,—Him whose office it is to lead them into all truth, and make real to them Jesus Christ the Son of the Father.

1. *Do you believe Him?* This is His pathetic plea to the disciples not only of that day, but of every day. "Believe also in me." "Believest thou not that I am in the Father, and the Father in me?" "Believe me .... or else believe me for the very works' sake." "I have told you .... that .... ye may believe." Oh, believe Him! How can you doubt Him? and your faith, though so little, is all he asks. Do you believe? Then your heart's trouble ceases. Then the peace He leaves with you is yours. Then you have the truth and the life, and are in the way. Then you know that the mansion is preparing for you and that He will come again to receive you to Himself. Then you recognize His claim, and honor Him and the Father and the Paraclete as one God. Then you are doing the "greater works" which, in the power of His Spirit, His disciples are enabled to accomplish. *Do you believe?*

2. *Do you ask in His Name?* Do you know what it is to pray, pleading His merit, identifying yourself with Him, and your cause with His, counting on His intercession, living in His

Spirit, and, proving His promises, finding Him faithful? Our prayers should find answer; do yours? If not, enter His school of prayer and learn this first and last lesson of the Christian life.

3. *Have you received the Comforter?* or as we ought to say, for it means so much more, the *Paraclete?* that is, the Holy Spirit, "One called to our side," who is our Helper in all things,—the One who may be called on in every need, for every grace. Have you received Him? Not only in baptism, but also through Word and Sacrament in a believing heart, again and again, in abiding, increasing, richer, fuller measure? The world cannot receive Him, but He is the believer's most blessed Gift and Portion. Is He yours?—comforting, teaching, leading, bringing to your remembrance the things of Christ? There is no more important question than this. He came to you in your baptism, and many a time since then through His Holy Word. Did you receive and welcome Him? Is He abiding with you? Is He in you?

4. *Do you love the Lord?* Not in mere words and empty protestations, but by the Master's test? Are you keeping His commandments? "He that hath my commandments and keepeth them, *he it is* that loveth me." "Many shall say in that day, 'Lord, Lord,' and I shall

say, 'I never knew you.'" Will He say that to you? Oh, our life, the life of the children of God, is one in which the law of love and liberty is the will of God in Christ. And this, not because we *must*, but because, out of our Spirit-filled hearts, we long and love to please Him. What is the law of your life? Do you ask, "Is it pleasant?" "Is it what I want to do?" or do you only wish to know whether it is what He would have you do? Blessed the man who loves Him in deed as well as in word, for He says, "My Father will love him, and we will come unto him and make our abode with him." That is enough. Come, Lord Jesus?

Prayer. O Thou, Who in Thine hours of bitterness didst think of me, Who couldst not leave me orphaned,—Lord, I believe, help Thou mine unbelief. In Thy Name alone I plead, and Thou wilt do for me! Oh, give me ever more fully, by Thy chosen means, the Holy Ghost, that He may work freely within me! And do Thou, O Christ, come with the Father, to let me be Thy dwelling place. Teach me to love Thee more, to keep Thy words, to do Thy will. Grant me Thy promised peace, and keep my heart from fearfulness, for Thou art my hope and my joy. *Amen.*

Tuesday after Reminiscere

I am the true vine, and my Father is the husbandman. Every branch in me that beareth not fruit, he taketh it away: and every *branch* that beareth fruit, he cleanseth it, that it may bear more fruit. Already ye are clean because of the word which I have spoken unto you. Abide in me, and I in you. As the branch cannot bear fruit of itself, except it abide in the vine; so neither can ye, except ye abide in me. I am the vine, ye are the branches: He that abideth in me, and I in Him, the same beareth much fruit: for apart from me ye can do nothing. If a man abide not in me, he is cast forth as a branch, and is withered; and they gather them, and cast them into the fire, and they are burned. If ye abide in me, and my words abide in you, ask whatsoever ye will, and it shall be done unto you. Herein is my Father glorified, that ye bear much fruit; and *so* shall ye be my disciples. Even as the Father hath loved me, I also have loved you: abide ye in my love. If ye keep my commandments, ye shall abide in my love; even as I have kept my Father's commandments, and abide in his love. These things have I spoken unto you, that my joy may be in you, and *that* your joy may be made full. This is my commandment, that ye love one another, even as I have loved you. Greater love hath no man than this, that a man lay down his life for his friends. Ye are my friends, if ye do the things which I command you. No longer do I call you servants; for the servant knoweth not what his lord doeth: but I have called you friends; for all things that I heard from my Father I have made known unto you. Ye did not choose me, but I chose you, and appointed you, that ye should go and bear fruit, and *that* your fruit should abide: that whatsoever ye shall ask of the Father in my name, he may give it you. These things I command you, that ye may love one another.

The Test of Love. The only reference to His passion which the Lord Jesus makes in this day's portion, is in the verse, "Greater love hath no man than this, that a man lay down his life for his friends." And then He says, "Ye are my friends." Most of us would assuredly shrink from such a test of friendship, still more when those for whom we were to show this wonderful love were not friendly to us, but even enemies, fierce and cruel and utterly unappreciative—still more if the agonies and bitterness of the death we must die were more and heavier than the sum-total of all human sufferings could be, a million million deaths in one! For that Divine One who took humanity upon Him, suffered out of the infinite capacity of His divine nature; because of this union of the divine with the human in His marvelous Person, He suffered tortures of heart and mind and body that were infinite,—so that His suffering and death are of infinite worth, and more than suffice for our every need. Thus "He laid down His life for His friends," taking their place and penalty, to free them from their fate. Oh, that we could count the worth of love like this! It is inestimably precious.

Sublime Messages. These parting words of Jesus, spoken in the upper room that last evening, are strangely beautiful. Each phrase is like a gem, and you need to turn it this way and that, to catch the lights it flashes from many an angle. All that has association with His sufferings,—promises, commands, exhortations, teachings that come out of His last days of earthly trial,—seem marked by a mysterious sublimity that sets them apart, alone.

The Vine. One other thing needs to be noticed of Him here. It is the relation He claims to all souls that have spiritual life. A branch cannot have life apart from the vine; and He is the vine. The life sap is in Him. Vital touch with Him, ingrafting into Him, this is the chief thing. Again it is clear that herein He claims what it were blasphemy for any mere man to claim. He is the vine, the life source, the uniting bond, the sustaining and fructifying root-spring of the whole.

As we meditate to-day we find before us questions that are peculiarly heart-searching.

1. *Are you a branch in Him?* That is, do you abide in Him? The question may seem hard to answer. Most of us think of abiding in Jesus as a high attainment, the acme of long endeavor. But it is not so. To abide is the simplest, easiest thing. A babe once put within its mother's arms can abide there. It cannot do anything else, wherever you place it, but abide. The Master enjoins upon us this relation of mutual abiding. He expects it, He

commands it. A comparison of John 6: 56, with this passage sheds much light upon the question of abiding. There it reads, "He that eateth my flesh and drinketh my blood, abideth in me." (Revised Version—The Greek word translated "dwelleth" is the same as "abideth" here in John 15.) A study of the context shows that the eating and drinking here referred to is not that which we enjoy in the sacrament of the Lord's Body and Blood, but is that participation in Christ which every believer has, the life communion which exists continually, and not only in the reception of the Lord's Supper. Whoever habitually feeds by faith upon the Lord Jesus Christ, he abideth in Him. It is like the analogy of food. I do not need to be always eating, in order that the food abide in me and I in it. But if I partake of food at suitable intervals, it is incorporated into my body and I abide in it. Are you then abiding in Christ? It means, "Are you a true believer? Do you feed upon Him, in Word and Sacrament, in the communion which faith brings?" If so, then He never leaves you and you never leave Him. Sleeping or waking, thinking of Him, or working for Him, or occupied with the duties of the daily life, He is abiding in you and you in Him.

The answer to this question, if you recognize and claim all that is involved in it, gives the answer to the next question.

2. *Are you bearing fruit?* Read what these verses say about bearing fruit. A branch that beareth not fruit He taketh away. It is cut off. A branch that beareth fruit, He does not hesitate to prune it with the knife of trial, that it may bear more fruit. Bearing much fruit is the necessary result of a true abiding in Christ. Bearing much fruit glorifies the Father. It is all so clear and simple. That is what we are here for, to bear fruit. That is why He has redeemed and chosen and regenerated us, why He has engrafted us upon Himself, that we should bear fruit, much fruit, more fruit. What use is there for a branch of a vine, that does not bear? It is an essential failure. And what am I, or what are you, if we bear not the fruits of the Spirit (Gal. 5: 22) in our own lives, and if we bear not fruit in bringing other lives to Christ? So let us claim and show this proof of abiding. The Master, from the upper chamber, at the threshold of His agony, gives us this lesson.

3. *Do we appreciate His love?* So as to abide in it; so as to love one another by the measure of His love for us; so as to feel the wonderful honor that is ours when He says, "I have called you friends." Of all the heroes of the Old Testament, Abraham alone has that

proud title given him, "Friend of God." (James 2: 23.) But each child of the New Covenant has a right to it. "Ye are my friends if ye do the things which I have commanded you." How proud we would be to have an earthly monarch call us friends; how much better, to be called a friend of Jesus.

Prayer. Lord Jesus, Heavenly Vine, let me not be separated from Thee, for apart from Thee I can do nothing, and I desire, abiding in Thee, dwelling in Thy great love, to bring forth fruit for the glory of the Father. I have not chosen Thee, but Thou hast chosen me, and so I claim Thy promised gift of fruitfulness, of fruit that shall abide. Hear me and answer, O Thou Friend of friends. *Amen.*

Wednesday after Reminiscere

If the world hateth you, ye know that it hath hated me before *it hated* you. If ye were of the world, the world would love its own: but because ye are not of the world, but I chose you out of the world, therefore the world hateth you. Remember the word that I said unto you, A servant is not greater than his lord. If they persecuted me, they will also persecute you; if they kept my word, they will keep yours also. But all these things will they do unto you for my name's sake, because they know not him that sent me. If I had not come and spoken unto them, they had not had sin : but now they have no excuse for their sin. He that hateth me hateth my Father also. If I had not done among them the works which none other did, they had not had sin : but now have they both seen and hated both me and my Father. But *this cometh to pass*, that the word may be fulfilled that is written in their law, They hated me without a cause. But when the Comforter is come, whom I will send unto you from the Father, *even* the Spirit of truth, which proceedeth from the Father, he shall bear witness of me : and ye also bear witness, because ye have been with me from the beginning.

Love's Recompense. There is no parallel in history, to the fact that the King of Love, in the supreme manifestation of love, was despised, rejected, crucified by the people He came to save in the self-renunciation of immeasurable love. Pathetic beyond expression is that word of St. John in the first chapter of his Gospel, "He came unto His own, and His own received Him not." It goes much further than this in the lesson before us. "They hated Him without a cause." Bitterest hatred, love's recompense! It is true that "love begets love." "We love because He first loved us." But love also meets invincible hatred, for "they hated Him," who is Love. The missionaries of Christ in foreign lands, coming in all loving sincerity to those whom they desire to save, have often met suspicion, misjudgment, hatred, and even persecution unto death. That is a distressing experience. Multiply their love and their sorrows by the measure of the difference between them and their Master, and you will gain some conception of the bitter pain of Him who was "the man of sorrows and acquainted with grief."

He saw clearly that the mad, unreasoning hate with which Satan had inspired the world against Him would extend also to all whom He chose and who acknowledged Him. All of these disciples, if we may believe tradition, died the death of martyrs. The persecutions that followed the Church for more than two centuries were the overflowing of this unutterable wrath against His people. What a wonder it is, that more, far more, than any tyrant or criminal or reprobate was ever hated, Jesus, the Meek and Merciful One was hated. This is the perverseness of sin! Look at Him! Is He, beyond all others, the Loving One, and the Beloved? Yes, and He is also, beyond all others, the Hated One!

Christ and the Father. Fail not to notice here, also, how he claims oneness with the Father. "He that hateth me, hateth my Father also." They do it "because they know not Him that sent Me." He is no mere ideal of humanity, man and nothing more! As He is true, He is the Son of God.

This Son of God, although hated and rejected, has witness to Himself. The Paraclete who proceedeth from the Father shall bear witness. With wonderful grace and condescension, He will accept also the witness of the disciples and not theirs only, but that of all His children, to this day. And they testify that, of all the sons of men, He only deserved no wrath! for He was sinless and full of grace and truth.

1. *How do you feel toward Christ?* What is He to you? That question is the touchstone of human character. Whoso hates Christ hates God the Father, hates his fellow-men, hates purity and the highest good. To hate, nay, merely not to love with supreme devotion, the pure and perfect Christ, argues a depraved spiritual condition. For a man to realize that his soul does not lovingly and loyally respond to the beauty and moral power of the character of Jesus, ought to be enough to reveal to him,

like a flash of lightning, unsuspected depths of corruption. Do *you* love Him, or are you on the side of His enemies?

2. *What is your relation to the world?* and how does the world stand toward you? It is greatly to be feared that very many of those who are called by the name of Christ to-day, are not distinguished by this mark of discipleship, that *the world hates them*, because they are not of the world, but He has chosen them out of the world. If we are brave and strong enough to show the spirit of Jesus, to speak as He spoke, and to live as He lived, the world will hate us, in the measure in which our sphere of opportunity enables us to bear testimony against its spirit. But the line of demarcation between Christ's children and those of the world is often strangely hard to find! The world would often claim as its own, of its spirit, akin to it in life and aim, in word and deed, those whom the Church claims, but whom Christ would not claim! "Lord, is it I" of whom such things can be said? Shall it be only in this Lenten season that I stand firmly and clearly on Thy side?

3. *What witness are you bearing?* Every one of us is a witness. Willing or unwilling, we *are* testifying. The only question is, are we witnessing for or against Jesus? Our lives are intended, by His grace, to show to men who

read no other Bible, what the Christ-life is. Our mission is to reproduce, in all its imitable traits, the life of Jesus among the men of to-day. Such a life is the strongest testimony, far more effective than any other sermon, to what He is,—how pure and tender and undeserving of the enmity of the wicked world. Such will be the witness of every life in which the Paraclete,—the Strength-giver and Guide and Illuminer and Witness of Jesus,—is permitted to enter fully and to work freely. It is well for each of us to ask, Is my witness, the testimony of my life, for the honor of my Lord, or does it slander Him?

Prayer. O Christ of God, Thou Who art One with the Father, we look upon Thee as Altogether Lovely. Thou hast our love, oh, teach us to love Thee more; and though the world hate Thee and us, let our increasing love be steadfast! Help us with lips and lives to bear blessed witness to Thy power to save and keep all those who put their trust in Thee. Grant that we may rightly estimate Thy loving self-abnegation for our sakes; and be to us to-day and all the days, the King of Love! *Amen.*

Thursday after Reminiscere

These things have I spoken unto you, that ye should not be made to stumble. They shall put you out of the synagogues: yea, the hour cometh, that whosoever killeth you shall think that he offereth service unto God. And these things will they do, because they have not known the Father, nor me. But these things have I spoken unto you, that when their hour is come, ye may remember them, how that I told you. And these things I said not unto you from the beginning, because I was with you. But now I go unto him that sent me; and none of you asketh me, Whither goest thou? But because I have spoken these things unto you, sorrow hath filled your heart. Nevertheless I tell you the truth; It is expedient for you that I go away: for if I go not away, the Comforter will not come unto you; but if I go, I will send him unto you. And he, when he is come, will convict the world in respect of sin, and of righteousness, and of judgment: of sin, because they believe not on me; of righteousness, because I go to the Father, and ye behold me no more; of judgment, because the prince of this world hath been judged. I have yet many things to say unto you, but ye cannot bear them now. Howbeit when he, the Spirit of truth, is come, he shall guide you into all the truth; for he shall not speak from himself; but what things soever he shall hear, *these* shall he speak: and he shall declare unto you the things that are to come. He shall glorify me: for he shall take of mine, and shall declare *it* unto you. All things whatsoever the Father hath are mine: therefore said I, that he taketh of mine, and shall declare *it* unto you.

Forgetful of Self. Love is another word for unselfishness! The small, unloving soul, in trouble, or in view of death, forgets all about the others who may be affected with him, and remembers only himself, his suffering, his loss, and pities himself so deeply that he has no pity to spare for others. How splendidly heroic, how nobly brave,—above all, how marvelously loving is the meek yet majestic figure of the Master, forgetful of self in His care for these poor disciples who must be tried by His trials! He has spoken these things that they may not be made to stumble. He is filled with thought of the persecution, excommunication, even martyrdom which they must after a while undergo; and against the hour that is hastening, He has sought to prepare *them*. You would think He was to be free from any trials and persecution of His own. Yet He is about to drink from the bitterest cup that was ever put to lips.

Going Home. For the few moments in which He spoke the words we are studying to-day, He seemed to be willing to forget the agony and look beyond. He does not speak of scourge and nails, but He says, "I go unto Him that sent Me." No matter by how strange and fearful a road, He is going home, to His Father, and He strengthens His spirit just now by looking over the gulf of grief and gloom, to the land on the other side. How homesick He must have been after thirty-three years of exile in a world of sin and wretchedness and enmity.

In view of the blessed return that was so near Him, it even seemed strange that sorrow should fill their hearts, if they loved Him. Oh, linger, Lord, upon the blessed hope, let it give Thee all the strength it may for the heavy trials that are before Thee!

He is True God. Here also is another lesson of His divinity. He who can send the Paraclete, Himself divine, is God alone. He, of whom the Paraclete testifies, whom to glorify is His all-comprehensive mission, can be no less than God. He who hath all things that the Father hath, is co-equal with the Father, God Himself. The One who spoke these words is true essential God, of the same substance with the Father, or else He is an impostor and blasphemer. We cannot deny His Godhead and yet reverence Him as the best of men. Either He is God, or He is the worst of men. But His whole life proved Him true and good, so we believe Him for what He claimed to be.

1. A lesson *concerning the Paraclete.* From these passion teachings, hallowed by the sacred influences of our Lord's last days, we receive our fullest message concerning the Holy Ghost. The Lord chose this season when the heavy clouds were closing over Him, to bring into clearer brightness the conception of the Spirit, of whom men had known so little. Have you

studied and appreciated this teaching of the Master? Is the Paraclete to you, and in your life, what the words of Jesus teach that He should be? Have you appreciated His inestimable helpfulness at the value indicated by this amazing declaration of our Lord, "It is expedient for you that I go away, for if I go not away the Comforter will not come unto you?" Better than the visible presence of Jesus, under our circumstances of life, is the presence and indwelling of the Holy Spirit. It is a truth worth much pondering. Have you practically honored the Holy Ghost as Christ shows that He deserves to be honored? Have you not, possibly, even failed to think of Him as a Person, truly God, as much to be loved and adored as the Father and the Son? Perhaps you have been used to refer to the Holy Spirit as "it" instead of using the pronoun which Jesus uses in speaking of *Him* in this passage. Honor and acknowledge the Holy Ghost! It makes a difference in the power and blessedness of your Christian life.

2. It is well to meditate a little while upon *the promised work of the Holy Ghost*. Has he done this work for you? Have you come to God's way of thinking, instead of the world's? The world counts murder and theft and adultery as the great sins. It counts one's faith or unbelief as a very little thing, a trifle. But

the Holy Ghost convicts men of sin because they have not believed in the Son of God. God counts as the greatest sin, unbelief, or the refusal of trust, because it is the *root* sin. What do you think about righteousness? The world reckons its own righteousness, like civil integrity, or good works of benevolence, the righteousness that saves. It rests upon itself for justification, and counts not at all upon Christ. But God's thought is that the only hope of righteousness is connected with Christ, and with His presence at the Father's throne to plead the merits of His finished work for sinners. Not one word of *our* good deeds, but only of *His* righteousness, is found in God's plan to save us. Again, the world thinks little or nothing of judgment. If it believes in judgment at all, it is of a judgment far away in the future, which it little fears. God tells of a judgment already pronounced! The prince of this world *is* judged. Sin brings present condemnation, and a sinner has no escape from judgment while he lives in sin. What do *you* think? Have you been taught and convinced of the Holy Ghost as to these things? Do you believe in Jesus Christ, trusting Him for righteousness, and thus escape the judgment which rests upon the devil and his children? "God's thoughts are not our thoughts;" but His thoughts are the true ones. Think His thoughts after Him.

Prayer. Lord, I worship Thee in Thy glorious divinity. I acknowledge Thee with the Father and the Holy Ghost, as one God. I thank Thee for Thine unselfish love, for the redemption Thou hast purchased with Thy blood, for the righteousness Thou hast obtained for me, and for the precious gift of the Spirit of Truth to take these things of Thine and declare them unto me. In my gratitude I offer myself unto that gracious Holy Spirit, for Him to lead and teach me ever to glorify Thee, O Christ my All-in-All! *Amen.*

Friday after Reminiscere

A little while, and ye behold me no more; and again a little while, and ye shall see me. *Some* of his disciples therefore said one to another, What is this that he saith unto us, A little while, and ye behold me not; and again a little while and ye shall see me: and, Because I go to the Father? They said therefore, What is this that he saith, A little while? We know not what he saith. Jesus perceived that they were desirous to ask him, and he said unto them, Do ye inquire among yourselves concerning this, that I said, A little while, and ye behold me not, and again a little while, and ye shall see me? Verily, verily, I say unto you, that ye shall weep and lament, but the world shall rejoice: ye shall be sorrowful, but your sorrow shall be turned into joy. A woman when she is in travail hath sorrow, because her hour is come: but when she is delivered of the child, she remembereth no more the anguish, for the joy that a man is born into the world. And ye therefore now have sorrow: but I will see you again, and your heart shall rejoice, and your joy no one taketh away from you. And in that day ye shall ask me nothing. Verily, verily, I say unto you, If ye shall ask anything of the Father, he will give it you in my name. Hitherto have ye asked nothing in my name: ask, and ye shall receive, that your joy may be made full.

These things have I spoken unto you in dark sayings: the hour cometh, when I shall no more speak unto you in dark sayings, but shall tell you plainly of the Father. In that day ye shall ask in my name: and I say not unto you, that I will pray the Father for you; for the Father himself loveth you, because ye have loved me, and have believed that I came forth from the Father. I came out from the Father, and am come into the world: again, I leave the world, and go unto the Father. His disciples say, Lo, now speakest thou plainly, and speakest no dark saying. Now know we that thou knowest all things, and needest not that any man should ask thee: by this we believe that thou camest forth from God. Jesus answered them, Do ye now believe? Behold, the hour cometh, yea, is come, that ye shall be scattered, every man to his own, and shall leave me alone: and *yet* I am not alone, because the Father is with me. These things have I spoken unto you, that in me ye may have peace. In the world ye have tribulation: but be of good cheer; I have overcome the world.

A Patient Teacher. Christ was a patient teacher. Most of us are vexed with the dullness of our pupils. But their "What is this that he saith, we know not what he saith," never made Him impatient, even though it grieved Him. One of the sorrows He bore was the spiritual stupidity of His disciples. Yet He saw that they were meditating, that they were inquiring into this question, and that was what He wanted them to do, so He set to work again and goes on to teach them further. A proof of His divinity is here. He foreknew that "little while" so full of grief and agony, and then of resurrection joy, when they should see Him again. How masterfully, like no human teacher, He goes on to explain what all this shall mean, and seeks to instill into their hearts some of the spirit that was filling and thrilling His, that of looking forward to the coming day when the travail should be passed, and be no more remembered for the joy!

He Speaks Plainly. Now, at their need, He speaks plainly and the deep under-surge of sorrow that we may detect through all these wonderful words comes to the surface again. He tells them of the hour when they shall be scattered and shall leave Him alone! He says that hour is come.

Not Alone. He says He is not alone; for so long as His Father was with Him He could not be alone! So it was, that through all that travesty of the legal trials, and the beating, and the nailing to the Cross, and the hot pulsing of the fevered blood as He hung beneath the fierce sun of the Syrian sky, He yet never felt the bitterest pain, never the uttermost anguish, until His Father's face was turned away from the Son who bore the sins on which God cannot look (Hab. 1). Then at last the awful cry rang out, so full of pathos, "My God, my God, why hast Thou forsaken me!" In that supreme moment when the full weight of our penalty was on Him, He was alone! alone!

1. More fully than before our gracious Master reiterates for us His promise of *the power of prayer in His Name.* By "that day," when they shall see Him again, He means not so much the day of His resurrection, as the day of the coming of the Holy Ghost,

His Revealer; in whom and by whose light, they should *see* Jesus and His work, understanding His Name as never before. In order to pray in His Name, more than all else do we need to live in His Name and love in His Name;—striving and hoping and having all our ambitions in His Name. The clerk, authorized to use his employer's name, is a feeble illustration; the wife who takes and uses her husband's name is better; but the son who receives help and encouragement and wins success in the name of his honored father, because he bears his name, is of his blood, and is one with him in character and aim,—this comes nearest to explaining how praying in the Name of Jesus means an identifying of ourselves, through His Spirit, with Himself, so that the Father, in hearing us, is hearing Him. Let us beware of emptying this word of its meaning, as though a mere saying: "In Jesus' name," at the end of our prayers should secure the promises; and let us question: "Do I truly ask *in His Name*?"

2. He bids us *be joyful*. He wants our joy to be made full. This is no gloomy life He calls us to lead. He passed through the gloom and bore the sorrows that our portion might be joy in its fullness. Are you joyful? Does your life in Christ beam in smiles, showing to every one who sees you that your Christ is a Joy-

giver? God forbid that we should, with gloomy aspect and sad demeanor, so misrepresent Him, that others, misled, will seek joys elsewhere! In Him is fullness of joy.

3. What a word is this of *the Father's love!* We do not need a Mediator as if our Father loved us not, but only because we are beloved in Him. He does not say that He will ask for us of the Father; He assures us that the Father loves us. Here is comfort. Think upon this: God loves you. Do not waste time in meditation on your love to Him, but ponder the thought of *His love for you.* All lies in that. If that be true there are no hard places in the Evangel, no mysteries that need cause stumbling. The problems of our sin and ill-deserving all vanish before this solvent. God loves me. "The Father Himself loveth you." He cannot help it, since we love His Son. You love those who love your dearest ones. So does the Father. Have you caught the preciousness of this truth?

4. Did He speak these words in vain, as to you? He spoke them *that we might have peace.* Have you peace? "Peace is joy made constant." Rest, quiet, gladness, unfailing sweetness in the love of God through Jesus Christ. It comes through Him, through His ransom, through His words. He desires so earnestly for you to have it. Let Him give it

to you. Let Him simply be all-in-all to you; live in Him, rest in Him, dwell in His love, and in the Father's love, abide in Him, He in you. It is not an acquirement, it is a gift. Being justified by faith we have peace. You have nothing of power or goodness, but you are able to take a gift. Even in the midst of the world we may have peace. Claim it.

Prayer. O Christ of God, so full of comforting and patient love, so self-forgetful, give us in Thee the Father's love and joy and peace, that all Thy blessed work and sacrifice for us may not be unavailing, but bring what Thou hast purchased for us, Lord, our Saviour. *Amen.*

Saturday after Reminiscere

These things spake Jesus; and lifting up his eyes to heaven, he said, Father, the hour is come; glorify thy Son, that the Son may glorify thee: even as thou gavest him authority over all flesh, that whatsoever thou hast given him, to them he should give eternal life. And this is life eternal, that they should know thee the only true God, and him whom thou didst send, *even* Jesus Christ. I glorified thee on the earth, having accomplished the work which thou hast given me to do. And now, O Father, glorify thou me with thine own self with the glory which I had with thee before the world was. I manifested thy name unto the men whom thou gavest me out of the world; thine they were, and thou gavest them to me; and they have kept thy word. Now they know that all things whatsoever thou hast given me are from thee: for the words which thou gavest me I have given unto them; and they received *them*, and knew of a truth that I came forth from thee, and they believed that thou didst send me. I pray for them: I pray not for the world, but for those whom thou hast given me; for they are thine: and all things that are mine are thine, and thine are mine: and I am glorified in them. And I am no more in the world, and these are in the world, and I come to thee. Holy Father, keep them in thy name which thou hast given me, that they may be one, even as we *are*. While I was with them, I kept them in thy name which thou hast given me: and I guarded them, and not one of them perished, but the son of perdition; that the scripture might be fulfilled. But now I come to thee; and these things I speak in the world, that they may have my joy made full in themselves. I have given them thy word; and the world hated them, because they are not of the world, even as I am not of the world. I pray not that thou shouldest take them from the world, but that thou shouldest keep them from the evil *one*. They are not of the world, even as I am not of the world. Sanctify them in the truth: thy word is truth. As thou didst send me into the world, even so sent I them into the world. And for their sakes I sanctify myself, that they themselves also may be sanctified in truth. Neither for these only do I pray, but for them also that believe on me through their word; that they may all be one; even as thou, Father, *art* in me, and I in thee, that they also may be in us: that the world may believe that thou didst send me. And the glory which thou hast given me I have given unto them; that they may be one, even as we *are* one; I in them and thou in me, that they may be perfected into one; that the world may know that thou didst send me, and lovedst them, even as thou lovedst me. Father, that which thou hast given me, I desire that, where I am, they also may be with me; that they may behold my glory, which thou hast given me: for thou lovedst me before the foundation of the world. O righteous Father, the world knew thee not, but I knew thee; and these knew that thou didst send me; and I made known unto them thy name, and will make it known; that the love wherewith thou lovedst me may be in them, and I in them.

The Lord's Prayer. This seventeenth chapter of St. John is the true Lord's prayer. What we call by that name is *our* prayer which He taught us, but this is His own prayer. It is a wonderful prayer. He asks first for Himself; then He pleads for His disciples who were there with Him; then for all those who should afterward believe on Him,—*for us.* He asks for Himself, that the Father should glorify Him. He looks forward to the agony on which

He is entering as the sphere and field in which He is to be glorified! So different are His thoughts from ours. We could have seen in it only shame and misery; He saw in it the glory of the Father, and His own. And He saw aright.

He claims wonderful things for Himself in this chapter—so simply, so naturally, not assertively, nor as if there were needed any proof of His claims. He declares that authority over all flesh is His; that He has accomplished, has perfected, the work committed to Him. He asks for that glory to be given Him which He had with the Father before the world was. He declares that He came forth from the Father, the literal words being very suggestive—"I came out from beside Thee." In the most clear and forcible way He asserts equality with the Father and Oneness with Him, when He says: "All things that are Mine are Thine, and Thine are Mine," and again,—" That they may be one as We are One"; "Even as Thou, Father, art in Me, and I in Thee." Such claims as these are worthy of our close attention and meditation. In these days of rationalizing conceptions, when men seem to honor Christ in one word and with another deny Him; when they offer Him the empty compliments with which they seek to cover the insult of their rejection of His true and essential Deity, it becomes us who love Him and who are jealous of His glory, to know just what He said of Himself, with His last words, in the full knowledge of His approaching end, under the solemnities of prayer and the sanction of communion with His Father. To deny that *He asserted His own true Godhead* is vain in the face of these and many other words. Far more strange than the great hidden mystery of His relation to the Father, would be the inconceivable mystery, that such an one as He shows Himself, in all His words and deeds, should falsely claim what He knew to be untrue, or should ignorantly assert what could not be. It is no avoidance of difficulty to deny the divinity of Christ, proclaimed as one of the chief among the passion teachings; it is on the contrary the undertaking of a far greater difficulty.

What Our Lord asked for His disciples then present He also sought for us in the words, "Neither for these only do I pray, but for them also that believe on Me through their word."

A tender thought is this of Jesus praying for us. What did He ask for his beloved children as His parting prayer? Let us see, and let the knowledge of His desires in our behalf move us to seek to realize their fulfillment.

1. He longed that *we should be one.* Yet it was not for a oneness of organization, as

many dream, but for such a oneness, in so far as possible, as that between Him and His Father,—a oneness of life, the one eternal life that He should give, a oneness of spirit, of love, of will. This must be fulfilled wherever true children of God are. It behooves us not to be striving after the union of church organizations, so much as after the oneness of the life of Christ. If we are one with Him, in His truth, in His spirit, in His purposes, we shall be, of necessity, one in all essential things with every other who is bound up with Him in the same unity. This is the best solution of the problem of Christian unity, that we be one with Christ and the Father.

2. He prayed that we might be *kept from the world's evil* even while we live in the world. Asceticism or monasticism was not Christ's thought for men. He wanted the light and the salt not to be separated from what they were to illumine and save, but to be in contact with it; but He besought the Father to protect His children from the evil in the world. Do you dread evil and fear evil and shrink from evil as He would have you do? Is this prayer of His being answered, so far as you are concerned? How is it in your business life, in your social life, in your daily contact, of whatever sort, with the evil of the world? Are you being sullied? And are you perhaps

careless, indifferent,—even lightly laughing at the sin that touches you on every side? Think of this prayer of Christ for you, and pray it for yourself.

3. He prayed that we might *be holy*, and pointed out the way to be holy. Do you earnestly seek to be holy, to be clean and pure, and to be living in the will of God? Do you love and use His Word, to this end? Is it a regular custom of your daily life to read and study the Bible for devotional profit? Do you delight to pause and think of the meaning of the verse you have read, then ask how it touches your life, and then turn it into prayer? Not only during the days of Lent, but every day, do you use the Word for cleansing and for growth? If not; if you despise and neglect the appointed means; how can you be holy? And if you are not seeking to be holy, how can you be His? Would it not be well to pause and pray for pardon just here, and then to promise Him with true repentance, to read the Word 'and to seek to grow in holiness through all the coming days?

4. He prays that at last we may be *with Him forever*. Here, perhaps, we have the most touching evidence of Jesus' love for us. He does not love us only with the love of compassion, but more, far more,—with the love of friendship. You can love, with the love that

sacrifices self to help and relieve, even the most hideous and wretched of men, yet that is far from meaning that you wish the companionship of that ignorant, degraded being in your home and by your side forever. But Jesus longs for us to be with Him, He wants us to see His glory, just as we like for our friends to see and share our happiness and the honor we have won. He desires us; He is not satisfied even in Heaven until He has us with Him. Oh, that is true love that lifts and glorifies its objects. How should we rejoice in it! He loves us with a surpassing love, with the love of a friend.

Prayer. O Lord, we are ashamed and humbled when we think of Thy divine condescension, and of Thy wondrous love. Fashion, shape and sanctify us until we shall be worthy of Thy heavenly companionship; and since Thou hast so dignified and honored us in our unworthiness, help us to be shielded and kept in all things, that we may not dishonor Thee,—until that glad day when we shall see Thee as Thou art, and shall be like Thee. *Amen.*

Monday after Oculi, which is the Third Sunday in Lent

When Jesus had spoken these words, he went forth with his disciples over the brook Kidron, unto the mount of Olives, as his custom was.

Then saith Jesus unto them, All ye shall be offended in me this night: for it is written, I will smite the shepherd, and the sheep of the flock shall be scattered abroad. But after I am raised up, I will go before you into Galilee.

But Peter said unto him, Although all men shall be offended, yet will not I. And Jesus saith unto him, Verily I say unto thee, that thou to-day, *even* this night, before the cock crow twice, shalt deny me thrice. But he spake exceeding vehemently, If I must die with thee, I will not deny thee. And in like manner also said they all.

The Hour has Struck. Though not yet delivered into the hands of his enemies, the Master has left the house of His friends, has spoken His last comforting and instructive words, and gone to the garden where His agony must begin. Past for Him are all the hours of peace, the unhindered communion with friends and disciples, the time of anticipation; come is the season of sorrow. He goes to meet it, not unconscious, but ready.

Very suggestive for meditation are the words, "*As His custom was.*" We think of Him here in His humanity; like one of us having His favorite retreat, like one of us becoming fonder and fonder, by use, of a spot at first attractive for some other reason. It is not unfitting that along with the reminders of His divine nature we should be impressed anew with His true human nature. A pleasant habit this is of seeking His chosen retreat to be alone, to commune with His Father. We can scarcely doubt that His custom was to seek it for the same purpose that brings Him here tonight: to pray. If He who was God so needed and so loved communion with His Father, how shall we live without it?

Consider the pity of it, as we enter into sympathy with Him in the garden, that His custom, so well known to the Twelve, made the task of the traitor the easier. He knew where the Lord was almost certain to betake himself, and he traded, in his treachery, on the knowledge that the friendship of Jesus had given Him. Baseness unparalleled!

As they went out, the Lord still had *a message of compassion* and forewarning. It is their bewilderment and helplessness in the face of the shock (for which all He says seems powerless to prepare them), that appeals to His pity. He would fain have them expect it, and be not utterly amazed when it comes. Though He remembers well that the Shepherd shall be smitten, it is the sheep, scattered abroad, of whom He is thinking and for whom He is caring. So, earnestly, He strives again to convince them of their weakness, and to drive them from self-confidence, that they may seek refuge in a higher help. But it is in vain! And the time of trial and stress is at hand.

1. There is a lesson for us in this *repeated warning* and *preparation*. Do we remember what He says to us? He had spoken often of His apprehension and death, as sure to come. This very evening He has repeatedly referred to these things as at hand. Now He says, "Ye all shall be made to stumble in Me this night." "The Shepherd shall be smitten." Again and again He had foretold the resurrection from the dead that was to follow; here also He makes explicit mention of it, saying He will meet them, after He shall have risen again, in Galilee. But they seemed not to hear, not to understand. And when the hour came for which He sought so earnestly to make them ready, they were as horror-stricken as if He had never foretold a syllable of what had so faithfully come to pass according to His word —they lost faith and courage, and were as thoroughly astonished at His resurrection as they had been cast down at His crucifixion. Do we understand much better what He has told us? When sorrow comes, many are as

deeply overwhelmed as if He had never said, "In the world ye shall have tribulation." When all seems to go wrong, and wickedness seems to thrive and fatten, we lose heart as readily as if He had not sent us the message of how men shall "rail at dignities," and "mockers come with mocking" (*Read 1 Peter, chapters 2 and 3*). He has intended that we remember and expect as certainly the promises of victory, as we find fulfilled His prophecies of evil.

2. *The Flesh and the Spirit.* How are we affected by these strong words of Peter and the rest, "Though I die with Thee, yet will I never deny Thee"? Shall we admire this sincere love and loyalty of purpose, or shall we wonder at the strange, unsuspected weakness of the flesh? A poor and pitiful thing is human nature, to vow sacrifice and martyrdom, when on the very verge of falling. We are of this same clay, honest in vowing never to deny the Master, yet with the willing spirit, weak, so weak of flesh! But even if men have endured trials as great as these, and even if we (which may God grant!) shall endure the temptations to denial of our Lord, it is by the rich grace of the Spirit whom He hath sent to dwell in and strengthen these poor powerless hearts. Swear allegiance to Him, but look to Him for strength to keep the vow.

Prayer. Dear Lord, we love Thee for Thy human likeness to ourselves, but most of all that Thou hast found a way, through bitterness and death, to make us like to Thee. We are so weak. Have pity on us and give us strength. We would not deny Thee, but Thou alone canst keep us true and faithful. Make us to hold in memory Thy precious promises, and evermore fully to entrust ourselves to Thee. By Thy holy passion, hear and answer us! *Amen.*

Tuesday after Oculi

Then cometh Jesus with them unto a place called Gethsemane, and saith unto his disciples, Sit ye here, while I go yonder and pray. Pray that ye enter not into temptation. And he took with him Peter and the two sons of Zebedee, and began to be sorrowful, greatly amazed, and sore troubled. Then saith he unto them, My soul is exceeding sorrowful, even unto death: abide ye here, and watch with me. And he went forward a little, about a stone's cast, and fell on the ground on his face, and prayed that, if it were possible, the hour might pass away from him, saying, O my Father, if it be possible, let this cup pass away from me: nevertheless, not as I will, but as thou wilt. And he cometh unto the disciples, and findeth them sleeping, and saith unto Peter, What, could ye not watch with me one hour? Watch and pray, that ye enter not into temptation: the spirit indeed is willing, but the flesh is weak. Again a second time he went away, and prayed, saying, O my Father, if this cannot pass away, except I drink it, thy will be done. And he came again and found them sleeping, for their eyes were heavy; and they knew not what to answer him. And he left them again, and went away, and prayed a third time, saying again the same words. And there appeared unto him an angel from heaven strengthening him. And being in an agony he prayed more earnestly; and his sweat became as it were great drops of blood falling down upon the ground. And when he rose up from his prayer, then cometh he to the disciples, and saith unto them, Sleep on now, and take your rest: it is enough: behold, the hour is at hand, and the Son of man is betrayed unto the hands of sinners. Arise, let us be going; behold, he is at hand that betrayeth me.

1. *Gethsemane!* What a synonym for the extreme of agony this word has become! The swiftly passing hours have brought Him here. He has come to the first battle-ground, the battle-ground with all in Him that cries out and shrinks with horror from the supreme sacrifice. Never was such anguish endured by another. Was the suffering even of the cross more bitter than this? Read the story again. Dwell on every word. See how sorrowful, amazed, sore troubled beyond comparison He is. Hear His bitter moans, such intensity of supplication! Thrice the entreaty to His Father! See the drops of bloody sweat pressed from Him, in His exceeding agony; and remember His abiding consciousness that now, almost at once, He is betrayed into the hands of His enemies. Nothing is spared Him of the utmost humiliation. The treachery that was so shameful and awful cannot be forgotten. He repeats the thought, "He is at hand that betrayeth Me." Read the story, and weep for this Most Innocent, suffering in your behalf.

Infinite Pain. This was no mere shrinking from the pains of bodily death. We sadly miss the meaning of our Lord's passion if we regard only the pangs of His human frame. The poison of the sin He was expiating gave infinite terror and pain to every moment of His suffering. Not the man alone, but the God-Man was in agony,—chiefly because the sin we esteem so lightly was revealed in all its awful depths of horror to Him who was sinless, who abhorred sin, yet bore it and claimed it as His own. When He, whose whole life had been apart from this deadly plague of the soul, who had fought incessantly against it, came to this hour in which He was to identify Himself with all the world's immeasurable weight of sin in order to free the sinners, He could not bear it at the first, He craved to be delivered from it. The Divinity in Him which enabled Him to be the Saviour made infinitely intolerable the pains and shudderings of His Spirit.

His Desire. One thing He craved: the human fellowship and sympathy of those who had been with Him. The solitary struggle He could not indeed share with another; but to know that His loved ones, the three who were nearest to Him, were watching with Him, were praying for Him; to come back for a moment from His lonely wrestling, from the horror of black darkness that was upon His soul, and find a ray of comfort in their tender, loving faces and their spiritual kinship, though they might have no word to speak,—this would have helped Him. It was denied Him. They who, a little while ago, had vaunted their willingness to die for Him, withheld from Him in this hour of need the poor comfort and support they might have given. They left Him utterly alone. Yet He had no bitter word for them, no stern rebuke. Poor weaklings, their spirits were indeed willing, yet they chose this time, of all times, to sleep. What helpless, worthless things we are at best!

His Prayer. Was there ever such prayer as this? All His agony, all His shuddering of soul, could not control His unswerving self-surrender to His Father's will. After the first awful crisis of unbearable distress, He ceases even to ask for anything; He accepts His Father's will without a desire of His own. "If this cannot pass away, Thy will be done." This brings rest, this is rest,—in whatever grief, to lie submissive, passive, not eager, nor striving, nor filled with desire, to lie all yielded to the Father's will, in the Father's hands. And the Father forgot Him not. Our hearts cry, "Thank God, Thank God," as we see the angel comforter. He is not utterly deserted. Thank God!

There is much for us in what we have already seen of Him. But there are other thoughts that bear more directly on our duty.

1. We ought to appreciate *the privilege of being chosen to fellowship with Jesus.* The Twelve had ever been honored in the choice of Jesus to nearest companionship with Him. The three,

Peter, James and John, the inner circle, that came nearest Him in love and in their understanding of Him, had been honored with special privileges, when He took them on the Mount to see Him transfigured, and when He took them into the maiden's chamber to see the little daughter of Jairus restored to life. But this was their highest honor, that they were chosen now to be with Him in His time of bitterness, to help Him in His anguish. They failed. They wearied, they slept. Oh, let us resolve, with God's gracious help, never to disappoint Him. Does He call us to service and to sacrifice in some especial way, near to His side? Is there a work to which He has chosen you,—to go abroad to bear His message to the lost ones of India, to enter His holy service in the ministry? as a deaconess? in some official station in the Church? in the Sunday-school? in the League? And you were thinking of refusing the call and shrinking from Him? Do not disappoint Him. Go from Gethsemane today resolved, whatever He wills, to do it. That one awful disappointment should be enough. God forbid that He should fail to find in you and me the trust and fellowship for which He looks.

2. Will it not be grateful to Him even now, in His glory, to receive from us the *sympathy with His sorrows* that He missed so

sadly on that awful night? Is not this one of the chief purposes of our observance of this passion season, that we may walk with Him in His path of agony, feel for Him, weep with Him, and pour out from our grateful hearts the offering of loving fellow-feeling that was denied Him then? Can we doubt that He will appreciate it to-day? You have your tears to shed over the sorrows of fiction, over the tragedies of history. Stop here awhile and enter into the woes of Jesus until your eyes are wet, and your heart grows soft with the fellowship of His sufferings, until your life is wrought into a deeper, tenderer communion with Him, a life-communion that shall endure throughout eternity.

Prayer. O Saviour, Who suffered the untold agony for me, give me a heart to feel Thy sorrows, so that all my stubbornness may become submission to Thy will, all my weakness strengthened into service for Thee, and my whole soul forever filled with self-forgetful, loyal love, centered in Thee: that Thou mayest fit and frame me for Thy gracious purposes, and I may never fail Thee, O Thou to Whom I owe life and salvation through Thine anguish! *Amen.*

Wednesday after Oculi

Now Judas also, one of the twelve, who betrayed him, knew the place: for Jesus ofttimes resorted thither with his disciples. Judas then, having received the band *of soldiers*, and officers from the chief priests and the Pharisees, and the elders, cometh thither, while he yet spake, with lanterns and torches and with swords and staves. Jesus therefore, knowing all the things that were coming upon him, went forth, and saith unto them, Whom seek ye? They answered him, Jesus of Nazareth. Jesus saith unto them, I am *he*. And Judas also, who betrayed him, was standing with them. When therefore he said unto them, I am *he*, they went backward, and fell to the ground. Again therefore he asked them, Whom seek ye? And they said, Jesus of Nazareth. Jesus answered, I told you that I am *he*: if therefore ye seek me, let these go their way: that the word might be fulfilled which he spake, Of those whom thou hast given me I lost not one.

Now he that betrayed him gave them a sign, saying, Whomsoever I shall kiss, that is he: take him and lead him away safely. And straightway he came to Jesus, and said, Hail, Rabbi; and kissed him. And Jesus said unto him, Friend, *do* that for which thou art come. Betrayest thou the Son of man with a kiss? Then they came and laid hands on Jesus, and took him. And when they that were about him saw what would follow, they said, Lord, shall we smite with the sword? Simon Peter therefore having a sword drew it, and struck the high priest's servant, and cut off his right ear. But Jesus answered and said, Suffer ye thus far. And he touched his ear and healed him. Now the servant's name was Malchus. Jesus therefore said unto Peter, Put up the sword into the sheath: the cup which the Father hath given me, shall I not drink it? All they that take the sword shall perish with the sword. Or thinkest thou that I cannot beseech my Father, and he shall even now send me more than twelve legions of angels? How then should the scriptures be fulfilled, that thus it must be?

Another stage in the matchless story has been reached, and Jesus is no longer in the hands of His friends, but a prisoner. As He spoke the closing words of the last lesson, one might have seen, under the branches of the trees, the glimmering of torches in the darkness. The scene was weird and impressive. He knew who the torch bearers were, and went to meet them. No attempt at flight, no endeavor to escape, no effort at concealment. Even these hard hearts must have been moved with admiration at the heroism of the One they came to seize. In the calm majesty of His dearly bought peace of soul, He speaks first, and asks them, "Whom seek ye?" They answer, "Jesus of Nazareth." The simple response, "I am He," is all that He utters. What strange power goes forth with the quietly spoken words? Surely some recognition of the fact that He is no mere man, must have touched their minds as they found themselves overwhelmed and driven back to earth, before Him, as by some invisible hand. And how Judas must have trembled! For there he stood at the head of the rough band. Again the question and the answer, and then

He asks for the freedom of the disciples who were with Him, thoughtful and careful, even in the very hour of His own arrest, not for Himself, but for them.

Judas might have spared Him that last indignity of using *the token of friendship* as the mark of His identity. But the baseness of the greed for gold, that can make even treachery possible, knows not where to stop. He had used his friendship, and the knowledge it gave him, for gain,—had traded upon it for thirty pieces of silver; what matter if he used friendship's holy seal and expression to indicate the One upon whom base, rough hands should fasten, that they might carry Him away to new indignities? Jesus understood him. "Friend," He calls him; and the soul of Judas must have writhed under the consciousness of his false friendship; then, "Betrayest thou the Son of man with a kiss?" Nowhere, in all these trying scenes, was Jesus deceived. He knew what lay before Him at every step. Judas had indeed betrayed, but not surprised Him. He *gave* Himself up to death. He was not a helpless victim. The stroke of Peter's sword in His defence was not in accordance with His will, so in His quenchless love, He healed the man who had come out to take Him. He was fully conscious of His power to escape. Celestial cohorts, legions of angels, were ready to speed down the pathway of the skies, if He would speak the word. How easily He could have saved *Himself!* But then had *we* been lost. He chose His own distress, and gave Himself up to die.

1. It is good for us to notice *the heroism of Christ.* Men have found goodness beautiful and attractive, but they have fancied it a more fitting attribute of the old or of the weak than of the young and strong. The goodness and gentleness of Christ have never been denied nor overlooked; it is well to ponder, too, the majestic manliness of Christ. He met these foes with that calm bravery which owes nothing to the artificial stimulus of the battlefield's excitement. He met them like an uncrowned king. With every woe and grief before Him, He was as free from fear as if the angelic legions were about Him, and He safe. Yet He was going to meet such a fate, fraught with such misery, as no other man ever met. This was a *man* upon whom you have been looking, —*a hero, a king of courage, a pattern of bravery.* Such a leader is worthy of the allegiance and admiration of the truest men of earth. Do not withhold your recognition. Be His followers!

2. There is *treachery to-day!* Again and again His followers are seen among His foes. In the world, in social life, on the exchange, in

politics, we find the disciples on the side of the enemies of Jesus. Men even use the Church and the Communion-table for personal aggrandizement,—yes, even to cover up and shield from suspicion their hidden lives of evil. It is the kiss of treachery. Is it not betraying Him, when we, whom He has loved, whom He has received into His covenant of friendship by our baptism, who have acknowledged Him as Master and Lord, in our confirmation vows, are found with those that hate Him? Is it not betraying Him when we sully the name we bear, by sinful lives?

3. It is a grand thing to be *obedient to the Captain*. Peter's stroke with the sword looked loyal and loving, but He would have shown more love and better loyalty, by waiting for the word of command. Futile and absurd was the unplanned, unauthorized, and unsupported attack. How vain the one sword wielded by the unskilled arm that struck only the ear, when he doubtless aimed at the head, in comparison with the twelve legions that only waited the Captain's word! Poor, weak, impetuous Peter. The Lord needed his companionship awhile ago, and Peter slept; the Lord cares only for his loyalty, now, and Peter flashes out a sword. After awhile this valiant defender will tremble at a maidservant's taunt, and deny his Lord. Oh, the great thing is not to be fighting, or

sleeping, or serving; the great thing is to be obeying—waiting for His Word, then doing His will. Be close to Him in spirit, in sympathy, in submission. Are you like Peter?

Prayer. O Thou, Who didst so nobly yield Thyself for me, let me not fail Thee in my courage or my faithfulness, but yield myself to Thee, for what Thou wilt. Be Thou my Captain, and I will obey Thy voice, O Thou Whose Word is power, and Whose heart is love! *Amen.*

Thursday after Oculi

In that hour said Jesus to the multitudes, unto the chief priests, and captains of the temple, and elders that were come against him, Are ye come out as against a robber with swords and staves to seize me? I sat daily in the temple teaching, and ye took me not. But all this is come to pass, that the scriptures of the prophets might be fulfilled: this is your hour and the power of darkness. Then all the disciples left him, and fled. So the band and the chief captain, and the *officers* of the Jews, seized Jesus and bound him, and led him to Annas first; for he was father-in-law to Caiaphas, who was high priest that year. Now Caiaphas was he who gave counsel to the Jews, that it was expedient that one man should die for the people.

And Annas sent him bound to the high priest Caiaphas, and there were come together with him all the chief priests and the elders and the scribes.

The Protest. It is to be noticed, here and afterward, that Jesus, either by words or by the rebuke of silence, protested against every step of the iniquitous proceedings by which the attempt was made to give an appearance of legality and justice to this predetermined murder of Him. Stern, yet calm and fair, was this arraignment of the brutal and cowardly arrest. Had He acted like a desperate and vicious criminal, that they should come to take Him under cover of darkness, by ambush, and with all the equipment of violence? Had

Himself or His work been hid away in secret places? Daily He had sat in the temple, teaching publicly, and they took Him not; nay, they dared not. The deed of darkness needed the hour of darkness and the power of the Prince of darkness. He could not more plainly have arraigned them as the willing and obedient slaves of Satan. And whether some fear of the supernatural might of evil that was arrayed against Him, or some inexplicable panic seized them now, it was at just this time that the poor disciples, who had boasted of their willingness and courage to die with Him, forsook Him, all, and fled. Deserted! He who would not desert them to save Himself! Not a friend beside Him, no angel now to strengthen Him! But there was no need. In the agony of the garden, and the submission of His soul there, He had put on the armor of proof, and He was strong. Deserted, yet He would and could walk on alone, through the griefs and shameful treatment that still awaited Him.

Before the Judges. They knew well where to take Him. The plot was all arranged. He should have no impartial hearing. He should stand before no judge who had not already prejudged Him. Quick, before the light comes, and the shadows flee away, and the honest sunshine shame them in their faces! before the disciples (too thoroughly despairing to attempt it) gather friends and succor Him! Quick, though all justice and honor forbade it, to the house of Annas, the father-in-law, friend, and fellow-plotter of Caiaphas; then to Caiaphas himself, most noble, upright judge, who had already given his verdict that it was well for this one man to die, and not that the nation perish! He spoke, unworthy instrument that he was, as the mouth-piece of the truth, yet he spoke in bitter, sinful hatred of the True One. And *he* is to decide this cause! O, Jesus of Nazareth, Thou art in the power of Thy foes, and Thy doom is fixed!

1. It is an awful thing to be *on the wrong side*. These priests and captains had won their purpose, and the Man of Galilee was their prisoner; but, none the less, He was and is the Lord, blessed forevermore, while they, in the very moment of their triumph, were prisoners of the wrath of God. They were defeated already, and He, in His manacles, was Conqueror. There is no victorious fighting against God. Often and often, God is *not* "on the side of the heaviest artillery." Lincoln was right when he answered to one who "hoped God was on their side," that the important thing was different, namely, that they should be on God's side. Let us find out on which side God is, and let us fight there; then are we sure to conquer.

God forbid that in anything you should be found fighting against Him. Where are you in the great battle of to-day? It is not hard for the earnest, unselfish, prayerful soul, to find God's side, Christ's side, in any question. Are you firmly resolved that, having found it, that is your side, at whatever cost and risk? If so, you are forever safe, and you shall win the victory.

2. Do we count the *Word sure and precious*, as Christ counted it? Two things we notice: He knew it, and He comforted himself in its fulfilment. Where another might have seen cause only for utter despair, He remembered that in the Scriptures of the prophets it had been written concerning their "hour and the power of darkness"; and if this was a part of God's plan, now in process of fulfilment, it was no ground for discouragement or despair, but only another proof of the truth and faithfulness of God, from whom He held many promises of precious comfort. So, if your sorrows and trials are part of God's plan for you; if you read in His Word of them, and of His needed grace to bear them, why are you cast down, why should you despair? Your trials prove His truth, as well as your joys! Trust in His Word and in Him.

Prayer. Lord Jesus, as we see Thee in the hands of Thy foes, we long to comfort Thee with the love and trust of Thy friends, whom Thou hast redeemed with Thy sorrows. While others fight against Thee, we long to be found on Thy side, and to share, if we may, Thy griefs, assured that we shall also share Thy victory. We would die for Thee, that we may live with Thee. We would endure, that we may reign with Thee. We would not deny Thee, lest Thou deny us. Pardon our sins, pity our weakness, and complete our redemption, for Thy Name's sake. *Amen.*

Friday after Oculi

And Simon Peter followed Jesus afar off, and *so did* another disciple. Now that disciple was known unto the high priest, and entered in with Jesus into the court of the high priest; but Peter was standing at the door without. So the other disciple, who was known unto the high priest, went out and spake unto her that kept the door, and brought in Peter, to see the end. The maid therefore that kept the door saith unto Peter, Art thou also *one* of this man's disciples? But he denied saying, Woman, I am not. Now the servants and the officers were standing *there*, having made a fire of coals; for it was cold; and they were warming themselves: and Peter also was with them, standing and warming himself: and the cock crew.

The high priest therefore asked Jesus of his disciples, and of his teaching. Jesus answered him, I have spoken openly to the world; I ever taught in synagogues, and in the temple, where all the Jews come together; and in secret spake I nothing. Why askest thou me? ask them that have heard *me*, what I spake unto them: behold, these know the things which I said. And when he had said this, one of the officers standing by struck Jesus with his hand, saying, Answerest thou the high priest so? Jesus answered him, If I have spoken evil, bear witness of the evil; but if well, why smitest thou me?

A Vivid Picture. A graphic story it is that you have just read. It must have come from the lips of an eyewitness. No wonder painters have often portrayed it: it is a word-picture. Simon Peter following Jesus, but afar off: John entering in while Peter stood outside by the fire of coals, warming himself,—these are simple touches that show how clearly, in after days, the whole scene, and all connected with it, come back to John, as he had beheld it on that ever memorable night. This narrative is no fiction.

The Investigation. Listen to the judge, before whom stands the Innocent One. The high priest asks of the teaching of Jesus. His answer is a manifestly simple one. He is there to be tried. They are the accusers, and it is their business to produce evidence. He only dwells upon the fact that He had done no underhand plotting (as had they). His work had ever been open and public. In synagogue or temple He had taught; let men who had heard Him testify. In this frequent public instruction many must have heard Him who could be easily found. As for Him, there was, as yet, no charge for Him to answer, so there was no necessity for Him to speak. Such a dignified and tenable position left the prosecution temporarily embarrassed. This procedure was indeed in the nature of a protest against the whole unwarrantable travesty of justice, yet it constituted no cause for just offence. But there was present one of those rude, coarse creatures who delight to be over-officious on the side that promises success, and rejoice in any opportunity to bully and oppress such as are in their power. Possessing a little authority as an officer (probably of the temple police), this fellow struck Jesus on the cheek with his hand, seeking thus to curry favor with his master, and asking, "Answerest thou the high priest so?" With marvellous meekness, but with the same unfailing refusal to suffer the wickedness and insolence of His enemies to go unchallenged, the Master, thus humiliated, gives an unanswerable response: "If I have spoken evil, bear witness of the evil, but if well, why smitest thou Me?" Was there ever such dignity with so great meekness? such brutal wrong done to spotless innocence? such shame, so mildly yet plainly reproved? The incident was significant. They had no answer; there was no accusation. For all defence of their unrighteous prosecution, they smite Him on the cheek. The cause that needs such vindication is the devil's own!

1. *A strange inner condition* is shown in the action of the two disciples that were following Jesus. Love would not let them turn utterly away, abandoning Him to His awful fate; fear would not let them take their stand by His side, and bravely avow their friendship. It could have helped Him none or little, had they been nearer to Him, yet following Him afar off was a dangerous thing to them. It is

impossible to know what would have come to pass if Peter's love had been stronger and His fear less. If, instead of making desperate and futile efforts to prove his ignorance of the famous prisoner, he had drawn near to Him, looked on His blessed face, heard the unjust trial, and seen the stinging blow, then it might have been that the memory of the warning, with the silent influence of his Friend and Teacher, would have kept him from that fearful fall. At least so much is plain, that there is no profit to Him or to us, in a half-hearted following of Jesus. Thorough devotedness, complete consecration, whole-hearted love and allegiance,—no less than this is His least due from us. How dare we offer Him less? Less is idolatry; for whatever we fear, love and trust more than Him is our God. That a man should deny Jesus seems to us now as strange and impossible as it did to Peter in the upper chamber, with the holy words still ringing in his ears; but it will seem easier, as it did to him, when foes are strong about us, when danger or mockery lies before those who confess Him. He only will be faithful, who has learned, before the time of stress,—like Daniel and his brave companions,—to let Him be first, and to give Him undivided trust and love. "Unite my heart, O Lord, to fear Thy name!"

2. Have *you* ever been *ashamed of Jesus?*

Have there been times when in words or deeds, or by silence, you have said: "I am not one of His disciples"? Do you expose yourself to such associations and temptations as may rob you of your courage, turning you into that most despicable and cowardly thing, a denier of his friend? It is easy to be ashamed of Jesus in the world of fashion and wealth, in the circles of a certain sort of culture, or amongst those who make a mock of the lowly Nazarene. But it is ignoble; it is unworthy of a true soul; it is a shameful thing! Open your heart to His Spirit, who makes men bold, and rejoice that you are not called to witness for Him with your life. Be loyal to the Kingliest of Kings!

Prayer. O Christ, if I deny Thee, it is not Thee alone that I shame, but my own soul. Give me the fullness of the Holy Ghost, that I may speak the word of witness, that I may do the act of faithful service, that I may be proud and glad, even where there are no others confessing Thee, to claim Thee as my Master and my Friend! For Thou art worthy, Who hast not denied me before Thy Heavenly Father, and Who didst give Thyself to make me Thine. *Amen.*

Saturday after Oculi

Now the chief priests and the whole council sought witness against Jesus to put him to death; and found it not, though many false witnesses came. For many bare false witness against him, and their witness agreed not together. And there stood up certain, and bare false witness against him, saying, We heard him say, I will destroy this temple that is made with hands, and in three days I will build another made without hands. And not even so did their witness agree together. And the high priest stood up in the midst, and asked Jesus, saying, Answerest thou nothing? what is it which these witness against thee? But he held his peace, and answered nothing. Again the high priest asked him, and saith unto him, I adjure thee by the living God that thou tell us; Art thou the Christ, the Son of the Blessed God? And Jesus said, I am: and ye shall see the Son of man sitting at the right hand of power, and coming with the clouds of heaven. And the high priest rent his clothes, and saith, What further need have we of witnesses? Ye have heard the blasphemy: what think ye? And they all condemned him to be worthy of death.

It is *a disgraceful task* upon which the religious leaders of the Jews have entered. There is no true witness to condemn Him, and the purpose is, not to give Him trial,—the purpose is simply to condemn Him. So they must have false witnesses. Word is sent out through Jerusalem. The high priests, who have paid blood-money to a wretched traitor, who have used cruelty and shameful injustice against a holy man, who have already condemned the innocent in their hearts, are now ready to add to these crimes, by undertaking subornation of perjury!

False Witnesses. Send out the word through the city,—"Wanted! false witnesses against Jesus of Nazareth, liars, perjurers! No honest man need apply! A good price will be paid to any one willing to sell his soul. Make application at the house of the high priest, Caiaphas." Many came, but, as is often the case with false witnesses, their testimony does not agree. Then send for others! Here come certain with a miserable perversion of words that He once spoke. The devil does not fail, even to-day, to use this same method of distorting and garbling a man's words, to make them mean another thing than what he said. These are most desirable witnesses, so bring them on! Alas! even their words will not agree! Something must be done. The high priest again undertakes to question the prisoner, their own Messiah, the Son of God. "What is it that these witness against Thee? Answerest Thou nothing?" Such tactics, in our courts of law, sometimes provoke an innocent man to such indignant reply as to prejudice his cause. Not so with Jesus. "What do these witness?" Plainly, they had witnessed nothing. So Jesus answered nothing. There was no accusation, no need of a reply.

The Important Question. Baffled again, Caiaphas adjures Him by the Living God to tell them, "Art Thou the Christ, the Son of the Blessed God?" Ah! here was a question He had come to earth to answer, and He will answer it. He said, "I am." Yet even now there are men who say that He never claimed to be divine, and that He is not divine. Let His words be set against theirs,—which is the liar? Then He added more,—"Ye shall see the Son of man [now so despised and scorned] sitting at the right hand of power, and coming with the clouds of Heaven." Quick of wit, the high priest saw his opportunity. With well simulated horror, he cried aloud, "No need of witnesses!" That was well, since they could find none with testimony fit to be considered. "Ye have heard the blasphemy!" He rent his clothes;—well if he had rent them in repentance for his own desperate and wicked deeds! "What think ye?" Now comes the answer: "Worthy of death!" So much of the farce is done. The sentence determined upon is at last extorted with a show of reason. Caiaphas, thou hast done well thy hellish task! It remains for those who call themselves Christians, and yet deny that Christ is the Son of God, to exonerate Him from the charge of Caiaphas. Either Jesus Christ is divine, or Caiaphas is right, and the prisoner uttered blasphemy! Join the rabble, and shriek with them before the Roman judge for His death, ye who deny His truth! But we will worship, and trust in Him, as in very truth God of God, Light of Light, and Lord of Lords!

1. Peter did well to fear, but he *feared the wrong thing!* How could a little maid, or a servant of the high priest, or a sword in his heart have hurt him, as the stings of his own conscience hurt him? or as the look of Jesus, —not vindictive, but full of pain and of reproach, when the cock's crow brought tardy remembrance of the awful sin. Ah! what fools we are to fear aught else than God and conscience. The awakening may come far later than with Peter, but surely one day, all who have denied and resisted Him shall meet His look bent on them from the judgment seat, and shall go out to weep and groan and gnash their teeth,—out into the darkness where no light of truth will ever come.

2. *Beware of prejudice.* It can turn a just man into an unjust; it can sap the sense of honor; it can lead to deeds the very thought of which would once have made us blush. Prejudice can induce the use of means that soil the hands of him that touches; it can degrade men who might have been noble; it can so blind the soul that no testimony will bring con-

viction. Caiaphas, if only he had deigned to give impartial test to the claims of Jesus at the first, might have found the truth. But he became the tool of Satan, and perhaps even compelled himself to believe he was doing God service. So much of selfish fear that he might lose power and influence entered into the formation of his prejudice, that he could not see the abominations of the course he took, "Better that one man die"? Surely not if you, through fraud and wickedness, must become His murderer. Oh, that we might give an open heart to the witness concerning our Lord! There is no unbeliever on earth, who, if he is willing to forsake the sins that hold him, and to give earnest, honest investigation to the testimony of the words and deeds of Jesus, will not be convinced. Touch the "honest skeptic" at the core of his heart, and you will find cherished sin, or else ignorance beyond excuse.

3. *He will come*, sitting at the right hand of power. Again, in these Lenten lessons, He speaks of His return. Before, to His friends, as a blessed comfort; now, to His enemies, as a terrible warning. Which will it bring to you —comfort, or terror? There is no better test of your heart's relation to Him, than the question, If He comes to-day, in His glory, in the clouds of Heaven, will you be glad, or horrorstruck? To Paul, His coming was a "blessed

hope." To Caiaphas, if he had believed the word, it would have been an unutterable dread. What is it to you? Can you, dare you say with John, in answer to the Lord's, "I come quickly," "Even so, come, Lord Jesus!"? That is the last prayer in the Bible. Is it yours? If not, then with true repentance, and with living faith, give yourself, this hour, wholly to Him, that, when He comes, you may be ready, and filled with joy!

Prayer. Dear Lord, let me never see that look bent on me, which Thou gavest to him who had denied Thee with oaths and curses. Let me never fail to hear and believe Thy words, "I am He," when they asked for Jesus of Nazareth; nor that "I am" with which Thou didst claim to be the very Son of God! Teach me to trust, more than I trust all else, Thy testimony to Thyself; and O Lord Jesus, when Thou comest, in Thy majesty and glory, may I behold Thee with confidence and gladness, and be caught up to meet Thee and to be forever with the Lord! *Amen.*

Monday after Laetare, which is the Fourth Sunday in Lent

Now Simon Peter was standing and warming himself. Then another *maid* saw him, and saith unto them that were there, This man also was with Jesus the Nazarene. They said therefore unto him, Art thou also one of his disciples? And again he denied with an oath, I know not the man. And after a little while they that stood by came and said to Peter, Of a truth thou also art *one* of them; for thy speech betrayeth thee. And one of the servants of the high priest, being a kinsman of him whose ear Peter cut off, saith, Did not I see thee in the garden with him? Of a truth thou art also one of them: for thy speech betrayeth thee: for thou art a Galilæan. But he began to curse and to swear, I know not this man of whom ye speak. And straightway the cock crew. And the Lord turned, and looked upon Peter. And Peter remembered the word which Jesus had said, Before the cock crow, thou shalt deny me thrice. And he went out and wept bitterly.

Increase of Grief. The sufferings of Jesus and the depth of His humilation were the more increased by the denials and oaths of that disciple who had seemed foremost in faith and in fervor. Though the Master knew what was coming, this did not lessen His grief on hearing His friendship made naught, and His very Name denied with curses. Peter had forgotten the special love and care which the Lord had manifested in warning Him, and in praying for

Him, so that the cock's crow was unnoticed the first time, and its reminder unheeded. How earnestly the Master had sought to caution both the traitor and the denier! The foretelling of the deeds they were about to do was intended, and should have served, to guard these men against the commission of such acts. The individual care of Jesus, and the high estimate He puts upon the single soul, is strongly shown in this, that He used prophecy, and gave such watchful and loving oversight to save Peter from his fall. Such is the worth of a poor human soul, that in the midst of His own sorrows, and at the time of these events of eternal import, He turns aside, first, to caution, then to watch, and then to remind His child, in the sin and peril of that fall!

He looked on Peter. A volume of meaning was conveyed by that look. Much of reproof, of reminder, and of sorrow, did it reveal to him upon whom it was bent. It carried the poor sinner, who had so weakly denied his Lord, back to the upper room, and he heard again the tender words spoken to forewarn him. In an instant it drove away all his cowardly fears by arousing that nobler fear of self and of his awful guilt. It caused him to see the great black gulf of seemingly hopeless condemnation, into which he had fallen. There was never such another look of wounded love, nor one so penetrating into the heart's depths of its object, nor so eloquent of reproof of sin!

1. *Easy is the descent into sin.* First, Peter follows afar off. Then he answers the question of the doorkeeper, a certain maid, and says, "I know him not." Now another maid asks him, and he reiterates the lie, swearing to make it stronger. Then *men* accuse him of having been with Jesus. A friend of the man whose ear he had cut off undertakes to identify him; and the poor, trembling disciple, who had been frightened by the maidservant's careless question, sees difficulty and danger thickening about him, and can devise no escape save by greater falsehood and more vehement oaths. Then the cock crowed for the second time!

2. *Sin is never solitary.* Peter's unbelief, like that of all the disciples, was a sin. The forgetfulness and distrust of the words in which the Lord had foretold all that followed, was the root-sin. His fear, arising from this unbelief, was sinful, and that led to the first lie, which was not only a lie, but also an act of cowardice, a denial of his best friend, an insult to Jesus, and a shame to his own soul. Then comes the added sin of perjury, of swearing to a lie, and taking God's Name in vain, and of cursing, wishing woe and uttering imprecations upon those who were accusing him. All this

brood of sins and vices grew one out of another. Who would have thought it of Peter? None less than Peter himself. Beware of sin, if for no other reason, because you cannot know where it will end.

Prayer. O Lord, give me a deadly fear of sin. If he who was so strong and zealous, could fall like this, what strength have I with which to meet the same foe? Oh, let me not, like him, be driven far from Thee! Thou art able to keep and to bless me. Let me never grieve Thee by denial of Thyself, or of Thy Spirit, whether in thought or word or deed. Keep me from trust of self, for I am weak and helpless. And in Thy love and mercy, endow me with the salvation which Thou hast obtained for me at cost of grief and loneliness. *Amen.*

Tuesday after Laetare

And the men that held *Jesus* mocked him, and beat him, and they did spit in his face and buffet him. And they blindfolded him, and asked him, saying, Prophesy unto us, thou Christ: who is he that struck thee? And many other things spake they against him, reviling him. And the officers received him with blows of their hands.

Now when morning was come, all the chief priests and the elders of the people took counsel against Jesus to put him to death. And the whole company of them rose up, and brought him before Pilate. And it was early.

Then Judas, who betrayed him, when he saw that he was condemned to death, repented himself, and brought back the thirty pieces of silver to the chief priests and elders, saying, I have sinned in that I betrayed innocent blood. But they said, What is that to us? see thou *to it*. And he cast down the pieces of silver into the sanctuary, and departed; and he went away and hanged himself. And the chief priests took the pieces of silver, and said, It is not lawful to put them into the treasury, since it is the price of blood. And they took counsel, and bought with them the potter's field, to bury strangers in. Wherefore that field was called, The field of blood, unto this day. Then was fulfilled that which was spoken through Jeremiah the prophet, saying, And they took the thirty pieces of silver, the price of him that was priced, whom *certain* of the children of Israel did price; and they gave them for the potter's field, as the Lord appointed me.

Mockery. Most men dread and dislike ridicule more than real pain. In order that Jesus might taste every sort of pain and indignity, He must also endure this. The Prince of

Heaven as the sport of rude servants is a spectacle for angels to weep over. They mocked Him, they spat in His face, they struck Him with their fists, and smote Him upon the face; then blindfolded Him and asked that He prophesy who it was that struck Him. And they spoke many things against Him, reviling. Royal sport, indeed, for these coarse-souled wretches! To spit upon purity, innocence, love, and self-sacrifice,—to find delight in torturing One who was so good and great and blessed,—this is fit occupation for the most brutal. We find new proof of the degrading power of sin, in this shameful exhibition. If there had been no Devil, this scene could never have taken place.

Next comes *another trial*. The formal sentence, according to Jewish law, could be pronounced only by day. So the whole Sanhedrin was assembled at dawn, and the blessed Lord was thither haled, to have the sentence already pronounced upon Him legalized. They have no idea of investigating His cause, but simply of making His condemnation formal. So they ask again whether He is the Christ. As He has done before, so now He protests against their prejudice and unbelief, showing how thoroughly He understands them and their purpose; but reiterates His claims to divine majesty, asserting what no mere man, what no one but God, could assert without blasphemy, that from henceforth He shall be seated at the right hand of the power of God. He also declares again that He is the Son of God; and then, for the second time, they condemn Him. At last,—for their utmost was done, and their power reached no further,—they bound Him and led Him to Pilate, the Roman Governor.

So far, among His own people, the Lord has witnessed *a good confession.* They have not been able to intimidate Him. Before their very rulers He has proclaimed His mission and His being. "His own" have rejected Him, and delivered Him for death to the power which, for their sins, had enslaved them. They must depend on the Roman government, which they hate, to perform their desire. To crush this Man, they will stoop to make use of any instrument.

Let us learn some lessons from the fate of Judas, as written in the lesson for the day.

1. *Sin goes much further than the sinner expects.* The awful dream of Judas is over, and gives place to a more awful awakening. The night he had spent has no description, but He had, evidently, kept himself informed of every step in the unfolding of the plot of the enemies of Jesus, and now, in the early morning, he learns that the sentence is death. Strangely

enough, it seems he had not expected this. And as he shrinks in horror from contemplating himself as the murderer of the One who had been ever so good and true to him, heart and brain together reel; he sees no doom too horrible for himself. Ah! if we could stop the influences of our sin when we would, it would all not be so fearful; but though it was easy for Judas to betray his Lord, it was impossible for him to undo the hideous deed. Who can say what memories thronged his brain?—recollections of the first days of companionship with Jesus; of the times of his own innocence of any evil thought or intention against Him; of bright hours that now only made his sin the blacker. The fate that he now saw so surely impending over the Master filled him with madness. But it was too late. He found no place for repentance, only for relentless remorse. Too late! Too late!

2. Sin's punishment lies partly in this, that its *rewards lose all their value.* What had he from this. irremediable crime? The thirty pieces of silver! Comfort yourself with them, Judas. They are as bright, and clink as merrily, and can purchase as much, as when you received them. Ah! as he looks at them, they are red with blood, they cannot purchase peace of conscience, they cannot buy back his innocence, they cannot redeem that life for

which they were paid! And so will every man who sells his soul through greed of gain, come to the hour when the gold that was so glittering, shall lose its glamour. Judas cannot keep his silver. Before the men who gave it to him, he hurls it down. But that helps nothing. Too late, too late!

3. The tempter has *neither help nor sympathy* for the lost soul he has ruined. Like a wail from the pit, sound the despairing words the traitor speaks in the ears of the high priests and elders: "I have betrayed innocent blood!" Does he imagine that his testimony will lead them to deliver the Innocent One? They knew His innocence as well as Judas. Will it impress them with pity for him, the traitor, when they had no pity for his Lord? Vain hope! Cold and impassive, they throw back on him his own responsibility: "What is that to us? See thou to that!" What is it to him who leads you astray, that life is blighted, and home is ruined, and hope for here and for hereafter is destroyed? "See thou to that!" What does the gambler care for his victim; the drunkard maker for ruined manhood; the rake for the woman he has despoiled? Look for sympathy from Satan, and when you have found it hell will have been abolished. Those who have led him to his fall, care naught for the despair of the lost one. So

Judas had no friend on earth, no friend in Heaven, and there are no friends in hell. Judas can no longer endure to live on earth, and he makes the awful leap. "He went to his own place." A lost soul, a ruined life,—no help for the evil he has done, no hope for him. Too late! Too late! Oh, the awfulness of sin! Once done, it is too late for any one save God to reach and hinder it.

4. *Look back* from this end, to the beginning. Once this desperate suicide was a smiling babe. Hate sin, since it can so ruin and degrade a human creature! It may have been lack of mother's love, or father's oversight that allowed the seeds of avarice and covetousness to take such root in the heart of this man that even the presence and words of Jesus could not uproot the deadly weeds. What care and prayer have you and I to exercise, lest the little ones of our homes come to the same eternal doom as Judas! Life is so deep and strange a mystery, how dare we live it apart from God? Let Him in Holy Baptism take and seal our children, and let us in godly home-life and by prayerful oversight, through God's appointed way, entrust them to His keeping, where only they are safe. Fear sin, hate sin, oppose sin, until He shall come and complete His work who was manifested to destroy the works of the devil. (1 John 3 : 8.)

Prayer. O Christ, we are afraid. Our enemy is so strong, we are so weak. We shudder with horror as we gaze at this awful abyss of shame, and realize that all sin is alike, its end so terrible. Defend us! Enwrap us in Thy love and care. Keep us for we cannot keep ourselves. And let us fear nothing with such abhorrence as the least slavery to sin. Deliver us, O Thou who hast died for us! *Amen.*

Wednesday after Laetare

But the Jews entered not into the Prætorium, that they might not be defiled, but might eat the passover. Pilate therefore went out unto them, and saith, What accusation bring ye against this man? They answered and said unto him, If this man were not an evil-doer, we should not have delivered him up unto thee. Pilate therefore said unto them, Take him yourselves, and judge him according to your law. The Jews said unto him, It is not lawful for us to put any man to death: that the word of Jesus might be fulfilled, which he spake, signifying by what manner of death he should die. And they began to accuse him, saying, We found this man perverting our nation, and forbidding to give tribute to Cæsar, and saying that he himself is Christ a king.

Pilate therefore entered again into the Prætorium, and called Jesus, and said unto him, Art thou the King of the Jews? Jesus answered, Sayest thou this of thyself, or did others tell it thee concerning me? Pilate answered, Am I a Jew? Thine own nation and the chief priests delivered thee unto me: what hast thou done? Jesus answered, My kingdom is not of this world: if my kingdom were of this world, then would my servants fight, that I should not be delivered to the Jews: but now is my kingdom not from hence. Pilate therefore said unto him, Art thou a king then? Jesus answered, Thou sayest *it*, for I am a king. To this end have I been born, and to this end am I come into the world, that I should bear witness unto the truth. Every one that is of the truth heareth my voice. Pilate saith unto him, What is truth?

And when he had said this, he went out again unto the Jews, and saith unto them, I find no crime in him.

The New Charge. "What accusation bring ye against this man?" We have reached another stage in His journey. He is now before a Roman judge, one not in sympathy with His accusers, and far from being their willing tool. What answer will they make to the question? —for, assuredly, He has broken no law of God or of the Roman Empire. Yet some answer has to be made. They will, boldly, seek to coerce Pilate by their unsustained assertion. "If He were not an evil-doer, we would not have delivered Him up unto thee." But this affords the Roman an easy way out of the difficulty. "Take Him yourselves, then, if it is some question of which our law takes no cognizance, and judge Him by your law!" But the true animus now appears, and they make response: "It is not lawful for us to put any man to death." He had already foretold, in prophesying His own death, a fate which seemed improbable; that He should be crucified. That was the Roman mode of execution. The Jews, when they had inflicted the death penalty, had used stoning. The narrator of the story carefully notes the exactness of the Master's knowledge of the event before the time!—But to return. Some accusation is necessary to lead Pilate to pronounce judgment on Him, and it must be one that shall have some weight with a Roman tribunal; so they lay the charge against Him of perverting the nation, and forbidding to give tribute to Cæsar, basing the slander on the specious statement that He called Himself Christ, which to their false conception of the office of the Messiah, meant king.

Pilate and Jesus. So Pilate questions Him. "Art thou king of the Jews?" Perhaps the prisoner will incriminate Himself. No; all that He speaks of is a strange kingdom not of this world, in which the citizens seek no victory with the sword, in which the kingliest office is to bear witness of the truth.

A strange scene! This earnest soul offering, even to the skeptical and superficial Roman, a glimpse of salvation. He does not disdain to declare His mission and His kingship to such an auditor,—bearing witness in the judgment hall of the Cæsars, as He had borne it in the palace of the high priest and in the temple, and wherever He might meet a human soul. There is no response in the breast of this hearer. The Divine Martyr has had to withstand the dullness of disciples, and the bitter hatred of antagonistic hearers,—now He must meet the sneer of skepticism. It is all very harmless, thinks Pilate;—incapable as He was of understanding and reverencing the kingly soul before Him;—merely an amiable fanaticism. This is not the sort of king that Cæsar need fear. But it is very foolish! The man is weak, perhaps a strong rebuke may help Him. "What is truth?" he scornfully asks; reflecting the fashionable philosophy of his day, which held that nothing is true, and that search for truth is fruitless. So speaking, he turns away. He has no time for such foolery. But he goes back to the accusers and declares that their accusation is not sustained. "I find no crime in Him."

1. Notice, in this passage, a characteristic of a *formal religiousness*. These men are daintily scrupulous not to defile themselves according to the outward precepts of their law, while lying and murder are staining their guilty souls. They could not put Judas' rejected silver in the treasury, it was not lawful. Did it not occur to these religious teachers that it was not lawful to pay it out, not lawful to purchase treachery and to make a prisoner of a guiltless man? That seemed a trifle to them. And here, murderous and perjured, they will not enter the judgment hall of Gentiles, lest they be defiled,—they, whose filthy hearts were already utterly hateful to Him whom they pretended to serve. Jesus had characterized them already,—"Straining at a gnat and swallowing a camel." How false they were! Accusing Him of perverting the people, raising a rebellion, forbidding tribute; while if He had really

done those things, they, vile hypocrites, would have applauded and assisted. He did not do them, so now with craven spirits they drag Him before the tribunal they detest, and seek to boast of their loyalty in taking His life. Yet never for a moment did they forget their ceremonial religionism!

This is characteristic of false religions—of all heathendom. It is characteristic of Rome. Persecution and all villainy are not sinful, but the mumbling of "Ave Marias" and the paying of penance dare not be omitted. It is characteristic of the human heart. You will not omit your saying of prayers, your presence at service, your outward compliances; yet you defraud, or you give place to greed in your heart, or you make little of true trust and love and fear of God, offering Him instead your empty formalism. If that is you, you are of the same family with these hypocrites before Pilate—and unless you repent you will spend eternity with them.

2. *Are you a citizen of this King?* Does your heart hear His voice? Do you love the truth, love not only to know it, but to live it? Is He King to you, and do you *serve* Him in this kingdom? Have you learned the answer to Pilate's question? Do you know Him as the Truth, and are you lovingly loyal to Him in the truth? Are you of the truth? Oh, the answer means so much! He wants not lip-

loyalty, but a heart filled with the truth, and a life that bears witness to the truth. Are yours like that?

3. What an awful thing it is to have, within you, *no response to spiritual things*. Here is the explanation of skepticism. It is the deadening of spiritual receptivity, which has progressed until, at last, the *truth* may stand before the skeptic, and not a chord in his soul respond. As well sing oratorios to a deaf man, or show museums of art to the blind, as to expect Pilate, and those like him, to appreciate and reverence the Christ of God. A soul dead to the highest things—God keep us from this fate!

Prayer. O Lord, our souls are hot with indignant sympathy for Thee,—tried, persecuted, belied, despised with the cool scoffing of ignorance. Let our fervor turn to love and make us earnest, faithful subjects of the truth. Forbid that we should miss the deepest, tenderest fellowship with all that is true and exalted, even with Thyself. Bind us ever closer to Thee through the sufferings Thou didst endure for us. *Amen.*

Thursday after Laetare

And the chief priests accused him of many things. And Pilate again asked him, saying, Answerest thou nothing? behold how many things they accuse thee of. But Jesus no more answered anything; insomuch that Pilate marvelled greatly.

And Pilate said unto the chief priests and the multitudes, I find no fault in this man. But they were the more urgent, saying, He stirreth up the people, teaching throughout all Judæa, and beginning from Galilee even unto this place. But when Pilate heard it, he asked whether the man were a Galilean. And when he knew that he was of Herod's jurisdiction, he sent him unto Herod, who himself also was at Jerusalem in these days.

Now when Herod saw Jesus, he was exceeding glad: for he was of a long time desirous to see him, because he had heard concerning him; and he hoped to see some miracle done by him. And he questioned him in many words; but he answered him nothing. And the chief priests and the scribes stood, vehemently accusing him. And Herod with his soldiers set him at nought, and mocked him, and arraying him in gorgeous apparel sent him back to Pilate. And Herod and Pilate became friends with each other that very day: for before they were at enmity between themselves.

And Pilate called together the chief priests and the rulers and the people and said unto them, Ye brought unto me this man, as one that perverteth the people; and behold, I, having examined him before you, find no fault in this man touching those things whereof ye accuse him; no, nor yet Herod: for he sent him back unto us; and behold, nothing worthy of death hath been done by him. I will therefore chastise him, and release him.

The Galilean Prisoner. How long the time of scoffing and mockery seems to last! Bitterly do His foes charge evil things upon Him. His silence amazes Pilate. But why should He reply until some wrong is charged against Him from which defense is needed? What evil has He done? A new indictment is alleged, more earnestly. "He stirreth the people up, teaching throughout all Judæa and beginning from Galilee even unto this place!" Pilate catches at the word "Galilee." A new humiliation for the Master is in sight. If He is a Galilean, Pilate may make use of Him. Herod and Pilate have been alienated. Why shall not the Roman at the same time get rid of a very troublesome case, and offer a delicate compliment to the Galilean King? That it is a fresh indignity and an injustice to the meek and silent prisoner, whom He has already twice pronounced innocent of any crime, is no reason to hesitate. So, as a peace-offering, he submits to Herod the decision of the cause between the Jews and Jesus.

The Galilean King. Another travesty of a trial! Again He is subjected to the shame of standing before a judge who is utterly unfit to exercise the office. Here Jesus meets a man who is so filled with empty and frivolous curiosity that his soul is incapable of receiving a serious impression, and the Lord casts no pearl of truth before him. To Herod, Jesus is no more than a showman, who can do some tricks by which he expects to be amused. Very greatly disappointed is he, that the object of his curious interest treats him with the dignity of disdain. Then, as they can extract no amusement from Him in any other way; since He declines to become a mountebank for their entertainment, and since the chief priests and scribes, vehemently accusing Him, must be appeased, Herod and his soldiers conceive the brilliant idea of making a huge joke of Jesus and His pretensions: so they mock Him, and set Him at naught, and put gorgeous apparel on Him; then, scoffing and jeering, send Him back to Pilate. Try to conceive of what all this meant to the soul so full of refinement, so conscious of the reverence due Him, and of the blasphemy they were committing against His Father!

Back to Pilate. Most unjust judge! Yet he is constrained to vindicate the Saviour. Again he testifies, "I find no fault in this man touching those things of which ye accuse Him. No, nor yet Herod, for he sent Him back to me, and behold, nothing worthy of death hath been done by Him." What then, Pilate? "I will therefore chastise Him and release Him." Why chastise Him, if He hath done no evil? That "therefore" leads to a lame conclusion. A *man* would have stood to the simple truth and justice of the thing. "Innocent, therefore released," should have been the verdict.

1. It is a great thing, sometimes, to be *silent*. So many men injure themselves by haste to speak. Notice the silence of Jesus. How eloquent it is! Plainly it tells of the emptiness and baselessness of their accusations; of His own courage and confidence; of the innocence of which He was conscious. Let us be silent when words could not avail, and when mere groundless malice seeks to hurt us. Let us "study to be quiet." Let us possess ourselves in silence, even when occasion is given for angry and indignant speech. Jesus knew when to be silent.

2. A man may be *glad to see Jesus*, and yet gain no profit. Herod was "exceedingly glad" when he saw Jesus. "Of a long time he was desirous to see Him." That sounds well for Herod. If you knew no more, you would feel very hopeful for the probable improvement of Herod's spiritual condition. But stop; why did he want to see Jesus? "He hoped to see some miracle done by Him." He wanted the Master to amuse him for a while. How many of those seeking to be Christians have need to ask earnestly the question, "Why do I want to see Jesus?" If it is merely for the sake of

custom that you wish your child to be baptized or confirmed, or that you yourself are about to take the solemn vows upon you; if it is because you will be thought of more highly, or can secure more easily some worldly purpose, then you deserve to be classed with Herod. He wanted Christ to entertain him: you want Him to assist you in securing some selfish end. He who, for his soul's good, and from love to the loving Christ, desires to see Him, will see Him unto salvation. To all others He will answer nothing until that last, awful day, when He will answer: "I never knew you!"

3. A pitiful thing is *a coward;* a man that knows right and does wrong. Here is Pilate, who declares, in the most positive way, that this prisoner is innocent, yet offers to scourge Him, in the hope that he will afterward be allowed by the mob to release Him. Compromises, for the most part, are born of cowardice. Pilate could have had no self-respect as he made this proposition. If He is innocent, you, as the judge, are bound to protect Him, and guarantee Him unhindered liberty. Now, as then, men are tempted to compromise conscience, to act the coward and the traitor to truth, for fear of offending those on whom they are supposed to be dependent. Yet it is hard to see how any man can look on this Roman weakling and afterward play the craven.

Prayer. Lord Jesus, I cannot fully enter into Thy sufferings, but my heart goes out to Thee. What wondrous love is Thine! What wondrous peace and patience! What long endurance, and what marvelous drinking of the cup! Help me to see Thee gladly, because Thou art my soul's hope. Deliver me from fear of man, and make me steadfast in the way of truth and justice. Help me, beholding Thine innocence, and Thy suffering, to trust and love and serve Thee fully. *Amen.*

Friday After Laetare

Now at the feast the governor used to release unto them one prisoner, whom they asked of him. And there was one called Barabbas, *lying* bound with them that had made insurrection, men who in the insurrection had committed murder. And the multitude went up and began to ask him *to do* as he was wont to do unto them. When therefore they were gathered together, Pilate said unto them, Whom will ye that I release unto you? Barabbas, or Jesus who is called Christ? For he knew that for envy they had delivered him up.

And while he was sitting on the judgment seat, his wife sent unto him, saying, Have thou nothing to do with that righteous man: for I have suffered many things this day in a dream because of him. Now the chief priests and the elders persuaded the multitudes that they should ask for Barabbas, and destroy Jesus. But the governor answered and said unto them, Whether of the twain will ye that I release unto you? But they cried out all together, saying, Away with this man, and release unto us Barabbas.

And Pilate spake unto them again, desiring to release Jesus; and saith unto them, What then shall I do unto Jesus who is called Christ, whom ye call the King of the Jews? They all say, Let him be crucified.

And he said unto them the third time, Why, what evil hath this man done? I have found no cause of death in him: I will therefore chastise him and release him. But they were urgent with loud voices, asking that he might be crucified. And their voices prevailed.

A Deeper Shame. Has not the Divine Sufferer already felt every sort of shame and sorsow that could be felt? Look back over the few hours since the exposure of Judas; Gethsemane, the travesties of trial, the spittings and smitings and rude mockery He has endured;—is there anything else possible? any new variety of shameful insult for Him yet to meet? Oh, yes, He has already laid aside His pride, or He would long since have turned back from this sorely painful pathway; there is yet greater humbling for Him to undergo. He must stand by, and see the heathen, the skeptical, the craven governor seek to save His life by making use of the yearly custom to set one free: He has to see this man plead for His release rather than for that of one who was leader of an uproar, a murderer and a robber. Oh, shameful conjunction of names! Barabbas or Jesus! "Which of the twain shall I deliver unto you?" Surely there can be no hesitation. Who would choose that a robber and murderer should be freed, and that such a spotless One as Jesus should be condemned? Yet He had to listen to the mad yell of the rabble: "Not this man, but Barabbas!" "They hated Him without a cause." "He came unto His own and His own received Him not." Depth of humiliation, to be pleaded for and defended by a stranger, a Roman, one of a hated race, and yet rejected by His own. Put into competition with a robber, and the robber chosen!

As Pilate asks: "What, then, shall I do

with Jesus, who is called the Christ?" for the first time there breaks upon the startled air, cutting to the heart of Him who has been bravely and calmly awaiting it, that awful, thrilling cry, "Crucify Him!" "Crucify Him!" "Why? what evil hath he done?" again asks the governor, who, if it cost him nothing, would fain release the Lord. "I find no cause of death in Him." And they cried, so much the more, "Crucify Him!" "Crucify Him!" Truly this is Satan's day, and the hour of darkness. Jews calling for the barbarous torture of the Roman's death penalty to be executed on one of their own race!—the purest One, the best One, the God-Man, the promised Messiah. Laugh, hell and devils, for this triumph is yours.

1. The awful sinfulness of *envy*. Envy is not commonly accounted one of the worst of sins, but no man knows what sin is, until he sees what it grows to, when unrestricted. Here is the fruit of envy. Pilate was right in his judgment of the real spirit that lay behind the malignant persecution of our Lord. The rise of Jesus meant the waning of the influence of these corrupt leaders of the Jewish people, and they knew it. Envy; hideous, ruthless, hateful, deadly envy, filled their hearts. Are you envious of those who are excelling you? Do

you feel jealous of the prosperity or popularity of those who may, by overshadowing you, make you seem less? Cut it out of your heart, if this evil is there, with the sharp two-edged sword of God's Word. It slew the Saviour. Full-grown, as we see it in this narrative, it means plotting, perjury, murder. It is a form of selfishness, therefore dig at its root, and by God's grace, be unselfish. Recognize the poison, and be filled with God's great antidote, *love*,—shed abroad in our hearts by the Holy Ghost. Be not of one mind with the murderers of the Master.

2. *Which do you choose?* Ah, you say you would not hesitate a moment between Jesus and Barabbas. But there is many another Barabbas. Between Jesus and ambition, which do you choose? Jesus or pleasure; Jesus or riches; Jesus or selfish ease; Jesus or self; which do you choose? Choose Jesus, Jesus always, Jesus only! and no curse, but a blessing, shall follow you forever.

3. Here is a foreshadowing of *the meaning of His death*. Barabbas is freed, because Jesus takes his place and goes to the middle cross, where *he* should have hung between the two other thieves. Barabbas in the place of the innocent one, Jesus in the place of the malefactor. A happy thing it was for Barabbas that Jesus was there to be crucified instead of

him; a happy thing for you that Jesus was crucified in your stead. For not Barabbas alone, but every sinner, was set free by the death of Jesus, on that terrible cross. This is a picture of redemption. Jesus takes the place due to me. I take the place due to Him. Only believe, and it is true for you.

Prayer. O Christ, the woe and horror and shame increase around Thee. Give me the sense of fellowship with Thee, for I choose Thee from among all there is to choose. I see Thee only, as the One to be desired. Thou hast willingly submitted to this shame and woe for me. I trust Thee, I love Thee, and I live in Thee. Use my life for the honor of Thy Name. *Amen.*

Saturday after Laetare

Then Pilate therefore took Jesus, and scourged him.

Then the soldiers of the governor took Jesus into the Prætorium, and gathered unto him the whole band. And they stripped him, and put on him a scarlet robe. And they plaited a crown of thorns and put it upon his head, and a reed in his right hand; and they kneeled down before him, and mocked him, saying, Hail, King of the Jews! And they spat upon him, and took the reed and smote him on the head.

Condemned! The voice of the mob had prevailed over the voice of justice and truth. No voice of manly courage had been raised. Jesus hears His sentence, and must bear from this time, in addition to the pain of every instant, the apprehension of all the cruel usages and awful agonies that lie between condemnation and the moment, long deferred in most cases, of the blessed release. But the brave heart knows its refuge and has found its peace.

First comes the scourging. Strip the prisoner to the waist; bind His arms about a pillar; find the most brutal of these hardened soldiers; bring the scourge, its leather thongs all knotted with sharp-pointed bits of steel and lumps of lead. Now, lay on! Once! Twice! How the tortured nerves and muscles writhe and twist, while our stripes are laid on Him!

Look; see how the streams of blood are trickling! Again and again the fierce strokes fall upon Him. Can you bear to look? How long can He endure this torture? Strong men sometimes succumb and die beneath the scourge, and He has had a sleepless night, has borne the agony in the garden, the shame of the arrest, and the five trials before as many tribunals. Will He sink? The barbarous beating still goes on. Oh, how can He bear it still? It is not finished yet for Him. He can not die until the cup is drained. It is not empty yet.—At last—it is over! The soldier who had wielded the hideous implement is wearied out. Now, surely, a little kindness will be shown Him. take Him to some couch, and spread soft cushions for Him, and leave Him a little while, that He may rest to gather strength for the way that remains to be trod. No! No! there is no rest for Him, who bears upon His bruised heart the sin of the world. These soldiers must have their sport. Bring Him into the judgment hall and send the word around. This is a joyous hour for these coarse souls that find their pleasure in unmanly, savage jesting with the miserable ones condemned to die. And this one offers peculiar opportunities for merriment. Look at Him! Does He seem a king? Sentenced to death, tottering with weakness as they bring Him in, stiff with the hardening blood-clots on His back, does He look a King? That is what He claimed to be. Cæsar's rival! Is He not an imperial figure? Ha! Ha! Tear off the rest of His garments. Here, throw over Him one of your rough purple cloaks,—that is near enough to the royal color to suit such an emperor as this. But He must have a crown. Run outside, some of you, pluck one of the common thorn bushes that grow around, and with your thick-skinned fingers, plait it into a crown;—it will not hurt you, but what sport it will be to press it down upon that brow of His, which, spite of all, holds such strange dignity upon it! Press it down. Jupiter! saw you ever the blood-drops spurt and trickle so from beneath the crown of the emperor? Ha! Ha! what a gladsome game this is! But He still lacks something. There stands a reed against the wall. Put it in His hand! Now He is robed and crowned and sceptred. Salute Him, comrades! Hail, King of the Jews! Did you ever hear such shouts of laughter? O! ye gods, what a gay hour is this! But He does not rave and rant and rebel as He should to make the joy complete. Smite Him upon the cheek! See if He will not wince! No? Then, here, see how He likes to be spat on! That bloody face needs washing. Snatch the reed from His nerveless hand, and bring it down upon His head! The crown does not seem to fit Him close enough. Drive it down the harder! What sport! Ha! Ha! hail, hail, all hail, thou glorious king! King of the Jews, all hail!

And amidst the hell-like laughter, the unseemly insults, oh, fix and carry the picture forever in your heart. The thorn-crowned King, majestic even in His humiliation! All this He bears for you. Oh, ransomed soul, can you forget it?

1. Could you believe, without this history, that man could be *so wretchedly debased?* That is sin. Never forget the picture. This that has gone before, this that you have just looked upon, all this that yet must follow, is sin. Hideous, horrible, it is sin. And will you love and serve it?

2. *How can our hearts be hard enough to witness this scene unmoved?* You who weep over the tales of fiction, will you not weep here? You whose hearts are stirred with indignation for wrongs far less than these, will you not be indignant for Him? And shall not your knees bend in sincerity of homage, before Him to whom those knees were bowed in mockery? Shall we not, with loving hands, wipe away the blood and spittle, and with tenderness embrace this scorned and despised Saviour? Oh, hard heart, melt, and offer Him your tribute of devotion!

Prayer. Lord, I am amazed at all Thou barest for me. As a sheep before his shearers, Thou wast dumb. I, too, am dumb before Thine awful agony. What shall I withhold from Thee, Who barest this for me? Receive my heart's allegiance, and my love. Lord, I will never scoff at Thee, nor scorn Thee. Let Thy love constrain me ever, till I see Thee in Thy glory as the King of kings! *Amen.*

Monday after Judica, which is the Fifth Sunday in Lent

And Pilate went out again, and saith unto them, Behold, I bring him out to you, that ye may know that I find no crime in him. Jesus therefore came out, wearing the crown of thorns and the purple garment. And *Pilate* saith unto them, Behold, the man! When therefore the chief priests and the officers saw him, they cried out, saying, Crucify *him*, crucify *him*. Pilate saith unto them, Take him yourselves, and crucify him: for I find no crime in him. The Jews answered him, We have a law, and by that law he ought to die, because he made himself the Son of God. When Pilate therefore heard this saying, he was the more afraid; and he entered into the Prætorium again, and saith unto Jesus, Whence art thou? But Jesus gave him no answer. Pilate therefore saith unto him, Speakest thou not unto me? knowest thou not that I have power to release thee, and have power to crucify thee? Jesus answered him, Thou wouldest have no power against me, except it were given thee from above: therefore he that delivered me unto thee hath greater sin. Upon this Pilate sought to release him: but the Jews cried out, saying, If thou release this man, thou art not Cæsar's friend: every one that maketh himself a king speaketh against Cæsar. When Pilate therefore heard these words, he brought Jesus out, and sat down on the judgment seat at a place called The Pavement, but in Hebrew, Gabbatha. Now it was the Preparation of the passover: it was about the sixth hour. And he saith unto the Jews, Behold, your King! They therefore cried out, Away with *him*, away with *him*, crucify him. Pilate saith unto them, Shall I crucify your King? The chief priests answered, We have no king but Cæsar.

Behold the Man! It seems strange that a Roman governor, and such a character as Pilate, should have taken so much trouble as he actually did to attempt the release of Jesus, yet without risk to himself. Partly it must be attributed to the message from his wife. Partly also, to the bearing and the mysterious influence of the Saviour Himself. At any rate, touched perhaps in his finer sensibilities with the aspect of the Lord after the terrible ordeal described in the last lesson, and hoping that the people would be touched with a like sympathy at sight of Him, he goes out again and asseverates his seven times reiterated judgment, "I find no crime in him;" then the tragic figure, still thorn-crowned and empurpled, comes forth, and Pilate with thrilling word and gesture cries, "Behold the man!" But bloodhounds know no pity. For all answer, resounds the now familiar cry, "Crucify Him!" Pilate is angered. "Take Him yourselves then and crucify Him. I cannot do it. Do it by mob law if you will, but I find no crime in Him."

Pilate's Superstition. They give a hitherto unmentioned reason why He should be put to death,—the Jewish law against blasphemy,—and assert that He deserves death (which they are powerless to inflict), "because he made Himself the Son of God." Strange compound of unbelief and superstition, Pilate remembers his wife's dream, and shudders at the thought that this man may have some magical, spiritualistic power, and that he may be bringing some curse of God upon himself. This must be looked into. So he takes Jesus back into the palace to question Him. "Whence art thou?" he asks. Again Jesus gives him no response. It is not for Pilate, moved with superstitious fear, to hear of His Divine Nature and eternal existence. The governor grows angry at this scant reverence to him, and threatens, "I have power to release thee and I have power to crucify thee." How strange the answer from the friendless Prisoner! The positions of the two seem reversed, as with the fearless dignity given Him by His own consciousness of the deeper meaning of the whole awful tragedy, the Martyr says, "Thou wouldst have no power against Me except it were given thee from above." Impressed, despite himself, by the manner and words of his Prisoner, and feeling, perhaps, more deeply than before, that His claim to be the Son of God must have some basis, Pilate sets himself the more earnestly to release Him.

Pilate Defeated. He little knows the craft and power of those with whom he has to deal. These shrewd adversaries threaten him with a charge of complicity with treason. Pilate did not want an investigation, by the imperial government, of certain of his acts that rose before his memory. A charge like this, entered against him at Rome, would be a very serious thing. His enemies and rivals might be able to use it to his undoing. Much as he desired to release Jesus, he was yet not willing, for honor, truth, and justice, to sacrifice himself. So he brings the patient Victim forth once more. He sees that he must yield. He will at least insult and flaunt those who have forced him unwillingly to this deed that shames him. "Behold your King!" he cries in mockery to the Jews. They knew how to drive the mockery back in bitterness upon himself. True, it involved hypocrisy and pretended loyalty to the rule they hated, but it will compel him if he still wavers. So they answer boldly, "We have no king but Cæsar!" "If thou release this man thou art not Cæsar's friend," still rings in his ears. He dares not shun the issue. He can make no further struggle. The rest is inevitable.

1. We should *pray for our rulers*. We are commanded to do so. In our general prayer, set for use in the public worship, we do so. It were well if we were more earnest in our pleadings in public and private petition. They need our prayers. Set in difficult places, surrounded by every sort of coercive influences, they may see clearly, as Pilate did, the right, yet feel themselves driven to do the wrong. God only can make men true to conviction,

brave to do right, and strong to persevere against every threat and loss. And, as we pray, we shall feel more and more our own responsibility for the elevation to high place of none but just rulers and judges, tried men and faithful. For woe to the land where Pilates sit on judgment seats! If men are to bear rule aright, those only must have authority who recognize the supremacy of the King of Kings, and of the justice and righteousness which He has decreed, and which are eternal. "God bless our native land," and make us "a people whose God is the Lord."

2. *Peace and confidence* come from the realization that wicked men and devils are under the control of Him who is above. Pilate had power because God permitted him to have power. Satan had power over Job only to the limit that God allowed. "The heathen rage, and the kings of the earth set themselves against the Lord and against His Anointed," but it is only so long as He shall choose, and to the boundary that He has set. To all the foes that may assail and do us hurt we can boldly say, " Thou couldest have no power against me except it were given thee from above." Thus we dare be fearless, for He who gives this power can take it away. "He causeth the wrath of man to praise him, and the remainder of wrath he will restrain." Why He permits

the use of this power, and what are His limitations on it, is His to know, not ours. Only believe. Trust in His love and might, and all is well.

Prayer. O Lord, *Thou* art my King, not Cæsar. Yet I do rejoice that in rendering unto my rulers what is theirs, I can render also unto Thee what is Thine. I pray Thee bless and govern those who govern us. Give victory to right, restrain the powers of evil, and hasten the good day when all Thine enemies shall be overthrown. Then, as we behold the Son of Man, who also is the Son of God, we shall not cease to praise and honor Thee for the redemption Thou hast given through Thy blood. *Amen.*

Tuesday after Judica

When Pilate saw that he prevailed nothing, but rather that a tumult was arising, he took water, and washed his hands before the multitude, saying, I am innocent of the blood of this righteous man: see ye *to it*. And all the people answered and said, His blood *be* on us, and on our children. Then released he unto them Barabbas whom they asked for: but Jesus he scourged and delivered to their will to be crucified.

And when they had mocked him, they took off from him the scarlet robe, and put on him his garments. And they lead him out to crucify him.

They took Jesus therefore: and he went out, bearing the cross for himself, unto the place called The place of a skull, which is called in Hebrew Golgotha.

Pilate has utterly yielded. If, in the human heart of Jesus, there had lingered a hope that the governor might be successful, it was dead now. That cowardly officer had washed his hands in public token that he was innocent of the blood of this just man, whom nevertheless he had a little while ago declared he could release. The people, mad with rage and self-delusion, had called down upon their own and their children's heads the blood they lusted for. Barabbas had been set free, and now Jesus is given over to their will. For the third time He is delivered over,—He who had from eternity received the adoration of angels,—to the mockery and sport of worse than brutal men.

Once more clothed in His own raiment, they lead Him out to another stage of His passion. Condemned, He now goes forth upon the *Via Dolorosa*, the grievous path. Whither? To Golgotha, name of ominous import,—the place of the skull. Bend those stiff and bruised shoulders for the last burden they shall bear on earth, O blessed One, with visage marred more than the face of any man. Thou despisèd and rejected of men, Thou man of sorrows and acquainted with grief,—bend Thy shoulder for this heavy burden, while they lay upon Thee the beam of the cross that is to lift Thee up so that Thou mayest draw all men to Thee! So "He went out bearing His cross for Himself."

To the foes who hated Him, what a moment of triumph as the last hope of help has failed, and the procession of the doomed moves forth! To Pilate, what a moment of hideous self conviction and sense of baffled effort, as he sees, or hears, the departure of the grim escort! To the timid disciples who may have been lurking on the outskirts of the throng, what a moment of anguish and absolute despair! To us, who love Him, what tenderness and sympathy bedim the eyes!

On the way to the cross, while every weary muscle aches, while heart and head and body are sick and like to fail! Through the familiar streets, catching here and there the fearful glances of triumphant hate and glee, guarded by the soldiers, and feeling heavier each moment the burden that so soon shall bear His quivering body in its utmost agony! Oh, the sadness of it!—the Lord of Life and Heaven bearing his cross for Himself, on the way to Golgotha!

Two lessons from this portion of the story:

1. *Water cannot wash away sin*, or responsibility. "Though I wash myself with snow-water and make my hands never so clean, yet thou wilt plunge me into the ditch and my own clothes shall abhor me." (Job 9: 30.) "Though thou wash thee with nitre and take thee much soap, yet thine iniquity is marked before me, saith the Lord." (Jer. 2: 22.) That were too easy a way to be rid of guilt. Condemn the just man to ignoble and undeserved death, and then call for a basin to wash your hands! Practice extortion and robbery, give yourself over to drunkenness and lust, put your Lord to an open shame, despise and neglect His Word and Sacraments, then, with the heart still unrepentant, take water and say, "I am innocent!" What a demand for basins there would be if Pilate's way were efficacious! He found it otherwise. Tradition tells of his miserable suicide on the mount that bears his name in Switzerland. It may be true, but if not, who doubts that he found throughout all his accursed

life the inefficacy of that water! No; if you have misused opportunity, if you have guilt and shame upon you, even the guilt of awful crime and vice, there is a place to wash. "There is a fountain opened for sin and for uncleanness." (Zech. 13: 1.) It is the fountain filled with blood. Who shall say that even Pilate, if he had come to repentance and to trust in the One whom he gave up to die, might not have washed there and have been clean? But there is no other way.

2. *God hears and answers the imprecations of His foes.* These men were not fit to pray, yet God heard their prayer and answered it. Down to this day a strange curse has rested on the people to whom He sent His Son, to be of their blood, and who received Him not. Through hatred and desolation and ruin manifold and persecutions unending, they have come with that blood, still insufficiently avenged, upon them and their children, even as they prayed. They live, their race unmixed with others, until the day when their blindness shall be done away, and they shall be saved through the Messiah whom they rejected; until the day when they shall look, with the look that brings life, upon Him whom they have pierced. God speed that day! And may He fill us with pity for them, that we may do our utmost to bring them to the Light of the world.

Prayer. O burdened Christ, as Thou goest on thy way, Take the sympathy and love of us for whom Thou bearest Thy cross! Make us to be clean. Wash us from our guilt. Fill our hearts to overflowing with abhorrence of the sins that made Thee suffer; and let us never lose the merit of Thy passion,—for Thy Name's sake. *Amen.*

Wednesday after Judica

And they compel one passing by, Simon of Cyrene, coming from the country, the father of Alexander and Rufus, to go *with them*, that he might bear his cross after Jesus.

And there followed him a great multitude of the people, and of women who bewailed and lamented him. But Jesus turning unto them said, Daughters of Jerusalem, weep not for me, but weep for yourselves, and for your children. For behold, the days are coming, in which they shall say, Blessed are the barren, and the wombs that never bare, and the breasts that never gave suck. Then shall they begin to say to the mountains, Fall on us; and to the hills, Cover us. For if they do these things in the green tree, what shall be done in the dry?

His spirit is still strong, but His flesh is growing very weak as the Master totters on. He must have fallen, or grown so faint that the executioner saw His powerlessness to stagger on, under the load He was carrying; so they impressed into this service a stranger, Simon of Cyrene, to bear the cross after Him. The procession begins again to move, Simon carrying the other and lighter end of the cross, which still rests on the shoulders of the Lord.

The Women Weeping. An incident which occurred, perhaps, during the momentary pause while the cross was being rearranged, has brought a new interest into the scene. Among the people, crowded around, were many women; some, doubtless, who had heard Him speak, perhaps had received great blessings from Him, either for themselves, or in the persons of those dear to them. Touched to the heart by the pathetic spectacle, they softened with their tears the path His feet must tread. It is the first manifestation of love and sympathy since His disciples all forsook Him and fled.

The Lord was not insensible to their compassion; His heart swelled with divine self-forgetfulness, and divine foresight of the future. He saw like an unrolling scroll the *awful days of the siege of Jerusalem;* the famine, the strifes, the unparalleled sufferings, which were to make this doomed people the most miserable on earth —the first considerable manifestation of the coming upon them in doom, of the blood they had invoked upon their heads. And He speaks with the cross-burden still on Him. In sight, perhaps, of Golgotha, He speaks to these women of the sorrows that lie inevitably before them, —for Jerusalem's day is past! He bids them weep for themselves. If the woe upon Him, the fruitful One, be so great, what will it be upon them, dead and dry, and fit for the burning?

1. Blessed service, to *bear the cross for Jesus!* Simon Peter, in this hour of the Saviour's need, was not there, though He had promised to follow Him even unto death. So another Simon

was found. The explanation which St. Mark gives, that he was the father of two Christians, well-known at a later time, indicates that this precious burden brought blessedness to Simon the Cyrenian. It always brings blessings to take up the cross and bear it after Jesus. Cross-bearing does not mean the mere acceptance of inevitable trials. Far otherwise. We may imagine that there must have been a sympathetic willingness to bear the cross of Jesus, which led to the selection of this man. It is certain that in the use of the phrase in the Scriptures, an involuntary bearing of an unavoidable burden is not to be understood. To bear the cross after Jesus means rather, to do what He did; that is to take up willingly the duty that demands self-sacrifice. The cross immolates self. The cross crucifies the flesh. The cross means service difficult to do, and self-denial hard to be borne,—and the willing acceptance of this service and practice of this self-denial, that alone, is taking up the cross and bearing it for Jesus' sake.

2. *The wages of sin is death.* The individual's sin brings the individual's death; the nation's sin, the national death. The punishment is sure, and when the "day" is past, the doom is fixed. To this city of Jerusalem shall come the vengeance she is now preparing. Where the cross stands now, shall stand the assailant's

tower. Instead of the procession going out of the gate, to slay the Innocent One, shall come great processions through the gates, and through the breaches in the wall, to put to death these guilty ones. He whom they have doomed to die because "all men run after him, and so the Romans shall come and take our place and nation,"—He shall be avenged by the coming of the Romans and the destruction of the city. Sin, unatoned for, means death. Where are your sins?

3. *Mountains and hills cannot cover guilt.* These Jews found it so when Jerusalem fell. Every sinful soul shall find it so, when the eyes of the Judge shall search him through and through. There is another day coming of which similar words are written. (Rev. 6: 12–17.) Oh, unsaved soul, beware! The mountains and the hills will be as ineffectual as Pilate's basin. There is One who can hide sin and cover guilt. (Read Jer. 50: 20.) Trust in Him. Make your refuge there.

Prayer: Lord Jesus, we pray Thee to give us strength to bear the cross and follow Thee. Since Thou hast borne it, our burden cannot be too heavy. Let our sins, crucified on the cross with Thee, have no more power within us or against us. O Lord, we hide in Thee, the Rock of Ages. *Amen.*

Thursday after Judica

And there were also two others, malefactors, led with him to be put to death.

And when they were come unto a place called Golgotha, that is to say, The place of a skull, they gave him wine to drink mingled with gall: and when he had tasted it, he would not drink. There they crucified him, and the malefactors, one on the right hand, and the other on the left. Then was the Scripture fulfilled, which saith, "He was numbered with the transgressors."

Golgotha. The end of the journey! The feet that have trodden, on missions of love and mercy, so many of the hills and valleys of Galilee and Samaria and Judæa, have taken the last weary path of His earthly life. The rest follows quickly. Since not every gleam of mercy is entirely excluded from these awful executions, they first stupefy the victims with a drink compounded of wine and myrrh, prepared, according to custom, by the women of Jerusalem. The two thieves drink it willingly, but Jesus will not take His departure with His senses dulled. He is here to suffer, to the last, all that is due the sinners in whose place He stands. He will drain to the dregs the cup His Father has prepared for Him, the cup of woe,—and so He will not drink of this cup of deadening. He tastes it, and perceiving what it is,

He puts it from Him. Think of the self-renunciation involved in this act.

The execution proceeds. Lay down the cross upon the ground, you who are appointed to this unenviable task. Stretch Him upon it. Now place the arms, extended, on the cross-beam. Hear, the nails and the mallet! More awful than the sound of falling clods upon a coffin lid, hear those blows, one after another, as the nails crush their way through tendon and bone in the palms of the hands, where meet and cross all the sensitive nerves that run from the fingers up the arms. What utterly indescribable torture He suffers! Place the feet, now, one upon the other, the sole of one foot flat upon the main beam; and with another large nail, forced down with heavy strokes, fasten them to the wood! Then lift up the cross; let its foot slip down into the hole dug to receive it, with a jar that hurls the body upon the pin that is to serve as a torture-seat, while every muscle is wrenched and strained until it would seem that the agony must drive Him mad. This is the penalty of sin. Every pain is intensified and made infinitely greater, because he who bears it is the God-Man, capable of infinite suffering, in order to cover the immeasurable sin of the world. "There they crucified Him." Simply the words are said, yet what horror of meaning they convey!

And, in order that no shame be lacking, not only is He executed as a criminal, and not only is the instrument of His punishment the shameful cross, but He hangs between two malefactors, one on the right hand and the other on the left. "He is reckoned among the malefactors." What a *terrible mistake* is here! The only man who never did an evil deed, never had an evil thought, never allowed a blemish or an error to stain His soul, is here on Calvary, reckoned a malefactor, dying between two thieves. The wild rabble looked at its work, while angels must have sobbed, if tears could be in Heaven, and devils must have filled the vaults of hell with madder glee than hell ever knew before. "There they crucified Him." His word has been fulfilled, and He is lifted up.

1. *Are you a sinner?* Then never forget that Jesus did not refuse to eat and drink with sinners, and in His last hour, to die with them. Nay, more, He freely died for them. The only ones who are excluded from His love and grace, are those who will not be reckoned among sinners. He came not for the righteous, but for sinners,—that they who feel their need, may find it supplied. Do not remain among those who love their sin. Let not those moments, prolonged into hours of agony surpassing speech or dream, be lost and wasted for you.

If never before, then now, here before the cross on which He has been fastened, let Him see of the travail of His soul for you, as, with true repentance and living trust, you give yourself to Him, to be redeemed!

2. He hangs *between heaven and earth*—and closes, thus, the broken circuit, that the grace of Heaven may freely flow through Him upon the sin-cursed earth. His arms are wide outstretched, as if to embrace between His pierced hands, the broad, lost world of men, and bring them close to His throbbing, love-filled heart. No other tree ever held aloft such fruit of life eternal! He is made a curse for us, as it is written, "Cursed is every one that hangeth on a tree." And since the curse fell on Him, the blessing that was His is ours! Have you touched Him, laid hold upon Him, that the current of the life of Heaven may course through you? Have you come within that wide-reaching clasp, and has His heart's love passed into your heart? Has this tree of death become to you the tree of life? Your eternity waits upon your answer. Let this contemplation of Him never leave you. In Him is life—and the life is for you!

Prayer. O God, in this Man, reckoned among the malefactors, is my pride and my hope. I will never glory save in this cross. I believe that on Him were all my sins, He bare them in His body, on the tree. And, since He bore my curse, oh, give me, in Thy justice, His righteousness and grace! Let me be crucified with Christ, that I may live; yet not I, but Christ in me. *Amen.*

Friday after Judica

And it was about the third hour when they crucified him. And Jesus said, Father, forgive them: for they know not what they do.

And Pilate wrote a title also, and put it on the cross. And there was written, JESUS OF NAZARETH, THE KING OF THE JEWS. This title therefore read many of the Jews: for the place where Jesus was crucified was nigh to the city: and it was written in Hebrew, *and* in Latin, *and* in Greek. The chief priests of the Jews therefore said to Pilate, Write not, The King of the Jews; but, that he said, I am King of the Jews. Pilate answered, What I have written I have written.

The soldiers therefore, when they had crucified Jesus, took his garments, and made four parts, to every soldier a part; and also the coat: now the coat was without seam, woven from the top throughout. They said therefore, one to another, Let us not rend it, but cast lots for it, whose it shall be; that the scripture might be fulfilled, which saith,

They parted my garments among them,
And upon my vesture did they cast lots.

These things therefore the soldiers did.

The *First Words from the Cross.* With His racked and tortured nerves tense with anguish, with the mockery and bitter hatred of His foes fresh in His memory, with long hours of continual pain, beyond expression, yet before Him, the Master opens His lips and speaks. What would you expect to hear Him say? Could any words of vehement rebuke be too severe for Him to utter after His long silence before the face of the tormentors? Will He denounce the wrath of Heaven upon their guilt? Will He speak words of might, bringing down fire from the skies to consume them? No; not so. He has no words for men, though He has thoughts in His heart of those who hate Him. He speaks to His Father. And the words? A prayer! For Himself, doubtless, in His utter weakness? No, not for Himself. For His friends, then, that they may be helped and strengthened, to bear their heavy burden without despairing? No, not for His friends. You and I would never have conceived it possible, without this sacred record, but it is nevertheless true, that the first words on the cross are a prayer for the forgiveness of His enemies. "Father, forgive them, they know not what they do." Ah, He is love! It will not do to say He has love, or that He is loving. This *is* love. He is not anxious, nor has He desire for Himself. Not His sorrows, but those of others, are on His heart,—and as He turns, now, from this most strange and awful place of prayer to the throne on high, He thinks of the abominable guilt of the men who have placed Him here, and fain would save them. Was any heart that heard this prayer so hard as to be still untouched?

The Superscription. A soldier climbs, to fix above His head the customary statement of the name and crime of the miserable one who hung beneath. A stir of curiosity goes through the multitude. What is the superscription? A moment, and every one can read it easily, for it is written in the three languages of which at least one was everywhere known at that day;— Hebrew, the tongue of the country, Latin, that of the Roman rulers, and Greek, the language of commerce and literature in almost every part of the known world. In these world-embracing languages, the superscription reads, "Jesus of Nazareth, the King of the Jews." How the high priests and their party raged! To brand them as subjects of that crucified malefactor! How it stung them, in their triumph. They demand that it be changed; that He be not awarded the title of King of the Jews; that, at least, it be written, "He said that He was King of the Jews." But the governor, smarting under their victory in securing the death of Jesus, was not to be moved in this point. He will not change what He has written, nor spare them one indignity that he has it in his power to give. So the Lord hangs tortured beneath the inscription that heralds Him King. The title they had denied Him is given Him on the cross.

Meanwhile, as part of their reward for their horrid service, the four soldiers beneath the cross of Jesus, are *dividing among them His garments*. One part they could not divide, for it was woven, and to tear it were to destroy it. Yet none was willing to yield it to his comrades. So, as had long ago been prophesied, (Ps. 22: 18), they cast lots. Mingled with the low groans of the sufferers, the indignant colloquy of the priests, and the awed murmurs of the spectators, might be heard the rattling of the dice in the helmet of a soldier, as one after another makes his throw for the seamless robe that had clothed the sacred body of the Christ, hanging above them.

1. Since the prayer of Jesus for His enemies, no man dare say he follows Christ while he keeps *an unforgiving heart.* Well does He practise what He had preached, "I say unto you, love your enemies, pray for those that despitefully use you and persecute you." And He taught us to say, "Forgive us as we forgive." Do you forgive? If not, you dare not pray in the public service of the church, or in your private chamber, the prayer He gave us. If not, you have not appreciated your own sin and the great forgiveness God has freely offered you. You are like the servant to whom the enormous debt had been forgiven, who took his fellow-servant by the throat and would have thrust him into prison, because he had not the means to pay the few pence he owed. If you dare to say in your heart "I will never forgive," whatever the injury you have suffered, then you are unforgiven, and dare not approach the altar with your gift. If any man have not the Spirit of Christ he is none of His; and Christ forgave His deadly foes.

2. God *wonderfully overruled* the speech and actions of men, in their relation to Christ. Prophetic meaning lies in the cruel words, "It is profitable that one man die, and the whole nation should not perish." And significant is the action of Pilate, in translating into all the tongues of the known world, the inscription for the cross of Jesus. It was true. In a deeper sense than he knew, he had written an imperishable testimony. This *was* the King of the Jews, foretold in psalm and story and prophecy, though now rejected; their King, though by them discrowned. Nor was He King of the Jews alone, but the Christ and the King for all the nations.

This was the first deed, while Jesus still lived on earth, betokening the world-wide meaning and interest of His mission. Every time we see the message, in Latin, Greek, and Hebrew, we are reminded that He is the Crucified Redeemer, for all the world, and our hearts bid us make haste to tell of His Kingship to every race, in every tongue,—unto every soul of man, to the uttermost parts of the earth. He said, "Other sheep I have, which are not of this fold; them also must I bring; and there shall be one flock, one shepherd." Is your heart with His, in this His great desire? What are you doing to tell of Him to the others, red, black, white, brown, for whom He died as truly as He died for you? In Africa, in Japan, in India, our representatives are seeking to fulfil the unconscious prophecy of Pilate in that tri-lingual superscription on the cross. Are you helping? Are you helping all you can and ought to help? Let us teach the nations to see this spectacle on Golgotha, and to read its meaning in their own tongue.

3. Even under the cross it is possible for men to be *greedy for self*, and in the idolatry of covetousness to forget the God who is dying above them. Beneath the very blood of Jesus the gambler will not forget the sorcery of his dice, while he has a chance to make sinful gain, though his prize be garments sanctified by the touch of Christ's pure body,—an offering of love from some who had supplied His lack of this world's goods, a seamless robe woven by some unnamed helper of the Lord. Let us beware of selfish aims intruding into our hearts even in the holiest places!

Prayer. O Christ instil within me the gracious spirit of forgiveness, that I may not withhold from any man free pardon like that which Thou hast given me. And use me, in Thy love, to tell Thy love to others. Hasten the day when every man shall have heard in his own tongue Thy saving Word. Let Thy love wean me from the things of earth, and Thy cross lift mine eyes above the greed of gain. *Amen.*

Saturday after Judica

And they that passed by railed on him, wagging their heads, and saying, Thou that destroyest the temple, and buildest it in three days, save thyself: if thou art the Son of God, come down from the cross. In like manner also the chief priests mocking *him*, with the scribes and elders, said, He saved others; himself he cannot save. He is the Christ, the King of Israel ; let him now come down from the cross, and we will believe on him. He trusteth on God; let him deliver him now, if he desireth him: for he said, I am the Son of God.

And one of the malefactors that were hanged railed on him, saying, Art not thou the Christ? save thyself and us. But the other answered, and rebuking him said, Dost thou not even fear God, seeing thou art in the same condemnation? And we indeed justly; for we receive the due reward of our deeds: but this man hath done nothing amiss. And he said, Lord, remember me when thou comest in thy kingdom. And he said unto him, Verily I say unto thee, To-day shalt thou be with me in Paradise.

The people stood gazing on. *Varied feelings* filled them. Anger mingled with the savage joy of the victorious yet unsatisfied priests and their followers; there was the natural, human pity of the more tender hearted among the multitude; and strange questionings arose in the minds of the thoughtful. The passers-by who turned to gaze upon the awful scene seem to have been fully in sympathy with the Lord's enemies, and not unwilling to add a pang to his sufferings; so they jeer at Him, and shake their heads, and challenge Him with taunts to prove His claims by coming down. Very hard it is to withstand such challenges when we are fully aware of our power to do. But Jesus seems unmoved by scorn. The high priests and scribes and elders, however, always ready to aid in such a work as this, add their voices to the scoffing of the rest, speaking in words strangely true and prophetic: "He saved others, Himself He cannot save." False as was the taunt that unless He came down from the cross He had no claim to be accepted as the Christ, the Chosen One of God, the King of Israel, yet in those first words they spoke truth; if He were to save the world He could not save Himself. This was the price He must pay. He had counted the cost and had made His choice. And easily as He could have vindicated Himself, even now, and come down from the cross, yet He could not save both Himself and us. He chose not to save Himself.

The contagion of mockery spread. Even *the thieves*, suffering, so far as the body was concerned, like torture with Himself, began to rail on Him; demanding that He prove his Messiahship by saving Himself and them. But to one of them comes some honest thought of what he is, and of what this Sufferer on the middle cross seems to be. He recalls many things, strange and impressive, that had taken place during the trial. Christ's bearing and His words even since they reached Golgotha must have moved him; as the prayer for the forgiveness of His enemies. Such divine unselfishness cannot be devoid of power even here, so this man turns from his scoffing to reason with his fellow-criminal, and then, humbly pleading, offers to the King on the cross the suppliant prayer: "Lord, remember me when thou comest in thy kingdom." Ah! here was something far better to the Saviour than wine mingled with myrrh, better than the compassionate tears of the women, best of all the joy and comfort that could come to Him out of the depth of His pain,—the first fruits of His passion, a soul longing for salvation! A pure, simple, beautiful trust, offered to Him whom all men were mocking. A repentant heart, surrendered to the One who so longed for the forgiveness even of His enemies. He forgets the pain and loneliness, and from this strange altar on which the bleeding Victim hangs He freely and joyfully gives full absolution to the waiting soul. He gives much more than was asked for! "This day shalt thou be with me in Paradise." *The Second Word from the Cross*, a word of life-giving. Joy on the two crosses! Joy in the soul of the Saviour over the lost that is found; joy in the soul of the forgiven sinner over the redemption he has gained. Joy in the presence of the angels over the one sinner that has repented. Even the agonies of death cannot keep Jesus from His work of saving the lost.

1. We should thank our Lord that *He did not accept the challenge* of the scorners. He had twelve legions of angels for his body-guard. Let Him speak the word of command. Let them speed, like lightning, down from the heavenly armories, and with glad hands set free their King and Captain in an instant. What silencing of the mocking! What release from pain for the Sufferer! What triumph and vindication of His claim! Yes; but to us, what loss! Our ransom lost. Our debt unpaid. Our guilt unexpiated. Our light turned into darkness. The heaven that was within our sight, eclipsed by hell. The bells ringing out our hope, changed into the tolling of our doom. Nay, He wanted no such triumph as this, which would have meant the failure of His mission. He chose rather the doom and the death, that in His apparent defeat He might gain the victory and fulfil the work He came to do. And we have to thank Him. Are you thanking Him, every day, with word and deed?

2. *Trust God* in spite of appearances. This seemed a natural challenge, and not only His

foes, but also His friends, doubtless felt that the argument of the scoffers was just. He said He was the Son of God. Would the Son of God be overcome by Jewish zealots and Roman soldiers? The Son of God on the cross? Who could think it? That weary figure, with nails through hands and feet, and hanging head, with blood-clots from the thorns still marking His brow,—that crucified criminal the Son of God? Who would believe it! If He is the Son of God, where is His Father? Let Him release Him. Grant that all seemed to disprove His claims. The argument was surely as strong as any argument of nineteenth century skeptics. Yet, spite of all, He was and is the Son of God, and He and His Father knew, though all the world was ignorant, why He hung there. Learn the lesson. However plain may be the seeming that God has forgotten you, it is only seeming. Trust God in spite of appearances, or you have no trust worth the name. Trust Him in the dark, or your faith is vain. Any one can trust Him in the sunlight. Do His will, and suffer His will, troubling not yourself about how it seems, and how men will speak of it. Jesus trusted Him, and left it to Him to vindicate His Son, and He did it, He will do it always.

Prayer. Dear Lord, Who on the cross

heard the cry of the repentant thief, hear the cry of my repentance now. Thy self-forgetting love, Thine immolation of Thyself for me, Thy patience and Thy meekness in the face of the scorn and the rejection of men, Thy grace in saving others, all have drawn my soul to Thee, —lifted up as Thou art on the cross. I praise Thee for Thy redemption. Help me to make my life, with all my thoughts and words and acts, "one grand, sweet song" of gratitude. I trust Thee and, through Thee, the Father, though darkness surround, and men despise and disbelieve. O Jesus Christ, Thou art the Son of God, and Thou hast died for me. What shall I do for Thee? Teach me to give the answer in heart, and daily life, until I shall see Thee as Thou art, and shall be like Thee! *Amen.*

Monday after Palmarum, which is the Sixth Sunday in Lent

But there were standing by the cross of Jesus his mother, and his mother's sister, Mary, the *wife* of Cleophas, and Mary Magdalene. When Jesus therefore saw his mother, and the disciple standing by, whom he loved, he saith unto his mother, Woman, behold, thy son! Then saith he to the disciple, Behold, thy mother! And from that hour the disciple took her unto his own *home*.

Now from the sixth hour there was darkness over all the land, the sun's light failing until the ninth hour. And about the ninth hour Jesus cried with a loud voice, saying, Eli, Eli, lama sabachthani? that is, My God, my God, why hast thou forsaken me?

Another comfort mingles with the exquisite anguish which is hastening to its culmination,—another, in addition to the joy of rescuing the thief. There are some near Him now, who love Him. How much it increases any grief, to be compelled to bear it alone! Even if the grief be beyond the reach of words, yet the silent sympathy, the loving presence, give some mitigation. So now, after these long hours throughout which He has been deprived of such comfort, there stand at the foot of His cross, His Mother with her sister Mary, Mary of Magdala (whom He had delivered from such sore bondage), and the disciple who loved Him best, John the Beloved. What a scene for a mother! Now were fulfilled the words which old Simeon had spoken to her when the babe lay in her arms: "Yea, and a sword shall pierce through thine own heart also." The sword was piercing her now, and oh, how sharp the pain! The Lord, in His own grievous agony, could not forget her grief, nor the love that had been lavished on Him throughout His life, and that found its mightiest expression now, in thus driving her here to share His pain while offering Him the solace of her beloved presence. He could not forget the years that lay before her in her widowhood and in her loss of Him. John, who had his own home, and was able to care for her, stood there. Some especial honor is due him, in recognition of his devoted affection and of his steadfastness in this last hour. So He speaks *the third word from the cross,*—a word of kindly provision for His loved ones,—as He gives to His mother a son whose heart was like hers in its unfailing tenderness to Him; and to the beloved disciple, the tenderest of all bequests, namely, filial care for the mother of our Lord.

Even in her bitter sorrow, we can still say to her to whom He gives His last thought of love, "Hail, thou highly favored among women!" He speaks: "Woman, behold thy son." "Behold thy mother." A new tie is formed; Mary finds a new home and a new son, whose loving relationship, sealed and cemented under the cross, will never fail her.

The end draws swiftly near; the awful culmination of the penalty for sin is at hand. God must deal alone, and in secret, with this One who has claimed the whole world's sin as His own. So He draws about Him the vail of a strange, mysterious darkness. From noon, for three long hours, the darkness lingers. The sun hides, ashamed and horror-stricken, at this scene: the wicked world crucifying its Lover and Saviour! And in His secret place, the Father enters into inquisition for sin. A terrible stillness marks this most dread intercourse. There are no words from Jesus. Those about Him, even the nearest and best, are incapable of comprehending what is transpiring. If a shudder of terror runs through the throng, it is not because they know what the midday twilight portends, nor what it hides. These were the hours of the utmost trial for the Lord, and at last, overwhelmed with the sense of remoteness from the Judge who, in His righteousness, is not able to look upon sin even when He who bears it is His Son,—at length the Saviour uttered, in His intolerable pain, *the fourth word from the cross.* It is a word of unendurable anguish,—"My God! my God! why hast Thou forsaken me?" This was the culmination of His woe, the acme of His punishment, that He had no longer the Father's presence, and the Father's approbation,—that, at this moment, the Son, doing His great, predestined, redemptive work, was lost in the Sin-bearer. So God saw not Him, but the murderers, the thieves, the adulterers, the blasphemers, the God-haters, the unbelievers, the sinners of every type and dye, whose guilt He had assumed as His own, and whose penalty must all be focused into this terrible time of the endurance of a misery which, though brief, was infinite in its intensity. The Sinless endured the abhorrence of His Father, that so Jehovah might look kindly on us sinful.

1. A sacred thing is *filial love*. If any son could rightly render only slight obedience and reverence to a mother, Jesus could have done it, for His Mother was a child of Adam, and a sinner like others; while He was divine and sinless. Yet He was always subject to her, and, on the cross, His love was shown to her most tenderly. How dare you or I then, to fail in our tenderness and loving provision for the mother who bore us? Son, daughter, are you forgetful of your mother and of her love? How are you repaying her suffering and sacrifice for you? Is your life such as to give her joy, or pain? Are you despising her love and piercing her heart with your waywardness,

selfishness, dissipation? Oh, beware! The Christ who, from the cross, tenderly cared for His Mother, will not forgive your irreverence and sin against the sacredness of motherhood. Repent and follow Him in this path also.

2. See *the courage of love*. The women loved Him more than the men who had followed Him, and they braved whatever danger there was in pressing near Him. Peter had seemed bolder than any, had spoken more, had professed more than John, but John loved more, and while Peter's courage had failed, John was with the women to receive the Lord's last trust. Oh, it is love that counts; love, that is the richest fruit of faith; love, which wins sacred commissions from Jesus; love, that gladdens His heart; love, that He longs for, from the souls for whom He poured out the unlimited streams of His own love. The strangest thing of all is that we love Him so little, that our love flames so faintly for Him. For He is most love-worthy. The severest indictment against a human heart,—the worst thing that can be recorded against it, is that it holds no love for the Most Lovable One, finds no response to His self-forgetting tenderness, is incapable of feeling the warmth of that great love which might warm the dead heart into loving. Do you love Jesus? More than earth's treasures or pleasures? More than

friends? More than self? How can we fail to love Him who is altogether lovely?

3. Who would be base enough to neglect or despise *the last trust* of a friend? Can you imagine John refusing or caring little for his duty of being a son to Mary? And yet, just before our Lord's last departure from earth, He gave *us* a trust: "the gospel of the glory of the Son of God, which was committed to our trust." (1 Tim. 1: 11.) Many have forgotten! He committed to us a mother, the Church, who nurtures and saves us. He called upon us to extend that Gospel and to sustain the Church, which He loves, and for which He died (Eph. 5: 25), until all the wayward ones are brought to her shelter, and the uttermost parts of the earth have learned of His grace! Are we keeping the trust? Are we cherishing His last bequest to us? Are we holding in sacred reverence, as our highest and most joyous privilege, the work He has committed to our care? Let the thousand millions of the unevangelized answer! What are *you* doing with this trust? That many are neglecting it, is clear. Are you guilty?

Prayer. O Lord, help me to love as Thou dost, to be tender, true, and selfless after Thine example. Forgive my unloveliness, and my lack of love for Thee. I desire to love Thee utterly and ever. Let no false love swerve me from full devotion to Thyself. Enable me truly and well to keep the trust Thou hast reposed in me. May I never lose the memory of Thy passion, nor miss its lessons for me. Lead me alway in the ways that Thou dost choose. *Amen.*

Tuesday after Palmarum

After this Jesus, knowing that all things are now finished, that the scripture might be accomplished, saith, I thirst. There was set there a vessel full of vinegar: so they put a sponge full of the vinegar upon hyssop, and brought it to his mouth. When Jesus therefore had received the vinegar, he said, It is finished! And Jesus, crying with a loud voice, said, Father, into thy hands I commend my spirit; and having said this, he bowed his head and gave up the ghost.

Still He lives and suffers on the cross. For many hours the Syrian sun has poured intense heat on Him, and the blood is running riot through His fevered body, while the increasing inflammation where tendons and nerves were so cruelly lacerated, creates within Him a burning thirst. Feeling these added pangs, He remembers how the Scriptures had foretold this, and He speaks *the fifth word from the cross,—*"I thirst." They give Him cooling drink, and the craving of His poor, tormented body is relieved: but there is a deeper thirst within Him. Like a hart, panting for the water-brooks, His soul is thirsting to draw near again to God, from whom our sins, not His, had separated Him. The hour is speeding now, when that thirst, too, will be sated. Yet there must have been behind this word still another thirst,—a yearning, too deep and full for a weaker word than thirst,—that the souls now perishing, for whom He was dying, should find life through His blood. That thirst is not yet slaked. You and I can help, by seeking to save others, in this giving of drink to Him. Are we doing it? "He shall see of the travail of His soul; and shall be satisfied."

Little cared He that some were still taunting Him, in their ignorance, with waiting for Elijah to come and help. For the cup was empty, now. What look He saw upon His Father's face; what messenger of Heaven whispered in His ear that eternal justice was now satisfied and our guilt fully atoned; or what inner knowledge He had of the coming of the end of the agony, we know not: but when He had drunk the draught of vinegar, the gladdest words earth or Heaven ever heard fell from His lips. "It is finished!" Thank God that the grief and pain of sin-bearing are finished, blessed Lord! Thank God that Thou shalt never need to suffer again for our redemption! Thank God that the manifestation of the Father's love and Thine, is complete; and so we can never fail to know that love for lack of its highest expression. Thank God, the plan and way of human salvation is finished, and there remains no whit to be done to make our ransom complete. The gladdest words that were ever spoken; for Him who spoke them, for Heaven that heard them, and for the world of sinners to whom the free gift of eternal life was announced in them! There was yet one awful spasm of pain; from his lips came one fearful cry; and the supreme pang was paid, His great heart broken. Like a weary child falling to sleep on the breast of its mother,—though thorns were His pillow, and the cross His cradle,—Jesus died. His last words were those He had heard at His mother's knee, or in the Bible school of the synagogue (Ps. 31: 5); words that have expressed the dying trust of Luther and of many saints—"Father, into thy hands I commend my spirit." No wonder men have said, "He died like a God!"

1. Let us realize the blessedness of a *finished redemption*. When men teach us that there is need of mediation by saints and martyrs we have but to remember the words, "It is finished." When they point us to penance, to fasting and self-mortification, as a means of adding to our merit before God, we need only recall the message, "It is finished." When they prate of a purgatory where we shall expiate our unforgiven sins, we can point to the expiation on the cross, and say, "It is finished." To trust in our prayers, our tears, our faith, our deeds, is to deny that He spoke truly when He

said, "It is finished." There is no other merit, no other satisfaction, no other hope than this of which He told us once for all, "It is finished." He will never make that sacrifice again on earthly altars by means of human priests; "It is finished." Nothing can stand between any human soul and God. All is done; "It is finished!" For us to accept the finished work, the complete redemption, is to receive its blessings, to live in Him forever. Let us not dishonor Him as if He had but partially and imperfectly done the work committed to Him. The music of His words will never cease; "It is finished."

2. He who does not with his whole soul respond to this awful sacrifice with trustful self-surrender is, of all ingrates, the *most ungrateful*. There is no sin so black, even as we count sins, as ingratitude. That one should imperil his life for you and not be rewarded with utmost thankfulness, is inconceivable. You would not receive an inestimable kindness from your fellow-man and then refuse him any grateful response that he would be willing to accept. If you did, your own heart would brand you base. Yet men who are honorable in earthly relations hear how He who yielded himself to redeem them longs for their trust and love, and turn their backs upon Him. Oh, that they would think what they do! Is ingratitude less shame-

ful because it is rendered to the God-Man who has died for us? And shall we withhold from Him aught, even the least of what we have and are, and call it less than shameful? All is His own, bought with His holy and precious blood, and with His innocent sufferings and death. Have you given Him the fullest consecration of your means, yourself, your heart and will? And dare you give Him less, since He claims it all?

3. When *God gave His Son*, He gave Him to this utmost agony, well knowing what He must endure. He gave him because He so loved the world. Let us not forget what it cost the Father's heart, as well as what the Son took on Himself. Let us count this one thing proved beyond a doubt,—God loves me! Whatever clouds may lower about me, whatever mysteries of chastening pain may visit me, whatever loss, bereavement, disappointment or sore sorrow may be my portion, I will never doubt, never forget that my Father once for all has proved to me His love, when He counted not His best and dearest too dear to give for my salvation! So, though I may not understand, I will not doubt. He loves me; though He slay me, yet will I trust Him. Be this the strength of my daily life, the comfort which I will whisper ever to my heart, God loves me. *God*, who gave His Son, loves *me*.

Prayer. Oh, Holy Lamb, slain from the foundation of the world, Thou that takest away the sin of the world, pour out upon me anew the blood that cleanses. Forget not my baptismal covenant with Thee; let its blessed privileges never be lost to me. And as Thy heart bled and broke for me, may my heart, purchased at this awful price, be only Thine. My heart is fixed, O God, my heart is fixed, and all my love and trust and service is Thine own, Thine only. I yield me to Thyself, and wonder that Thou art pleased to accept and use me as Thy child. Let my soul be lost in Thee. *Amen.*

Wednesday after Palmarum

And behold, the veil of the temple was rent in twain from the top to the bottom; and the earth did quake; and the rocks were rent; and the tombs were opened; and many bodies of the saints that had fallen asleep were raised; and coming forth out of the tombs after his resurrection they entered into the holy city and appeared unto many. Now the centurion, and they that were with him watching Jesus, when they saw that he so gave up the ghost, and saw the earthquake, and the things that were done, feared exceedingly, saying, Truly this was the Son of God. And all the multitudes that came together to this sight, when they beheld the things that were done, returned smiting their breasts.

Strange portents accompanied and followed the culmination of the great drama. At the moment of the death of Jesus, it was noticed that the heavily woven veil in the Temple, dividing the Holy Place from the Holy of Holies, was torn as by an unseen hand from top to bottom, so that the secret place,—hidden for centuries from the sight of every man but the High Priest, and seen by Him only on the Day of Atonement of each year, when he entered with the substitute blood to make reconciliation for the sins of the people,—this secret place was now revealed to the gaze of every one who looked. It was well. The age of ceremonies was past, that of realities was come. Types and shadows were no longer needed, for the substance was here. The blood of goats and bulls had no more virtue; the blood of the Lamb of God was shed. The separation between Heaven and man was done away and no veil could any longer keep the humblest and poorest from intimate communion with God Himself. The high priest of the old ritual was superseded; the true eternal High Priest had entered once for all into the Holy of Holies on high, and every believer in Him is himself a priest unto God. The ancient walls of division are no more. It was well that the veil was rent.

The old earth rocked and shook, as its Maker, lifted on its bosom, died in agony. The Centurion with his Roman soldiers, inured to every sort of strange and fearful scene, trembled and were afraid; in their amazement bearing testimony that "This was a just man, and the Son of God." The people who had witnessed all, now found, no matter with what feelings they had first come forth, a burdensome oppression fall heavily upon them, a melancholy apprehension of what all this might mean: and, recalling the darkness and the cry of Jesus (the like of it never heard from a crucified man before); feeling also the earthquake and the nameless influence that pressed like a weight upon them, they smote upon their breasts and turned away.

Such a scene could not be unaccompanied by supernatural, soul-thrilling incidents. He who had stilled the seas and calmed the winds and ruled the powers of nature in His life, could not suffer such an awful death and nature herself be dumb. Ah, you have cause to beat your breasts, ye dwellers in Jerusalem! Not many years shall pass till you have distressful cause to remember the spectacle from which, sad-hearted, you turned away.

1. Among the causes for gratitude that are inseparably bound together with the sufferings and death of Jesus, one of the greatest is that of which the *rent veil* tells us. We do not appreciate it, because we have never known what it is to have our Lord put far from us by earthly ordinances and priestly inventions. Perhaps, also, we do not know how to prize the blessing, because we have not with simplicity and faith made experience of it. But to a soul that has known only the darkness of heathenism or the twilight of Romanism, it comes as a truth quite fresh and wonderful, that the Holy of Holies is open to us because our own Mediator has, once for all, entered and bidden us enter. And to one who has made progress in the divine life and the full acceptance of its precious privileges, there is no richer joy than this; to press to the footstool of God and pour out in unre-

strained communion the heart's pleadings and confession. To be assured of the mercy and tenderness of God is inestimably blessed. To know that at every hour, in gladness and sorrow, in perplexity and anxiety, He is here, and that there is no veil between us; that we have only to look up, sure that He is looking down upon us; only to reach out the hand, sure that His hand is there to clasp it; only to go forward, sure that He goes by our side; only to ask guidance, sure that He will lead aright; only to confess our sin, sure that He freely pardons it; only to weep out our sorrow on His bosom, sure of His sympathy and of the balm He gives,—there is nothing more precious than this. But do you know it? Have you gained this communion? Is prayer your breath? Do you linger at the footstool, and wait and listen for the answer that He gives, while the Holy Ghost brings to your remembrance the words of Christ?

2. A pitiful *picture of the world* that knows not Jesus, is this which we behold—the people beating their breasts and feeling their burden, yet knowing no refuge, turning away from the Christ who is dead! If He had never lived again that would be the picture of us all. Like the two disciples on the way to Emmaus telling of their vanished hope and of their dead trust, would the highest and best of men have been.

There is, to-day, a vast multitude, who know their sin and poverty and wretchedness, but who find in Christ no life. The cross, to them, is but the place where He hung; and to them, He has never risen. So from the dead Christ of their disbelief they turn away; and, alas, too often they turn to the dark, deep-flowing river, or seek at the pistol's mouth surcease of sorrow, but seek in vain. Oh, tell them that though He died, there is life for us in the rich blood He shed; that He is not dead to-day; that He is the Life, and he who lives in Him shall never die; that in Him is righteousness and peace and joy. God grant that we may draw the wandering ones to Him!

Prayer. Lord of my life, let my faith not be less than the centurion's. Thou wast a Just Man, and Thou art the Son of God. Here, at the foot of the cross, where Thou hangest, let all of evil that is within me die. Here, as I stand and look on Thee, let the burden of my sin and sorrow roll from me. And as I live in Thee, may my life be full of Thy likeness; drawing, as the branch from the vine, all of its strength and fruitfulness from Thee. *Amen.*

Thursday after Palmarum

Read the lessons for the day: 1 Cor. 11: 23–32, and John 13: 1–15.

[The Gospel for the day has already been treated in our studies, (see page 40, Thursday after Invocavit), as also the account of the institution of the Holy Communion (page 51, Saturday after Invocavit). Therefore it has seemed well to include here a special meditation on the Lord's Supper, instituted on this Thursday evening.]

Matt. 26: 29. "I shall not drink henceforth of this fruit of the vine until that day when I drink it new with you in my Father's kingdom."

Our Lord had just instituted the sacred, mysterious, life-giving rite of the Holy Supper. He was supplanting, with this Sacrament, the old feast of the Passover. That had a typical lamb: this the anti-typal Lamb. That was an emblem: this was the reality. That was the lamb slain to foreshadow salvation through blood: this the Lamb slain to give redemption by His blood.

He had just said, "This do." In the same moment, He told them of the impending parting, and also of a reunion in the time to come. In the kingdom of His Father, after He shall have come again, we shall sit down with Him, to drink of the new wine. In the very moment of substituting a new feast for the old, He foretells that this, too, shall be done away. He would have us remember this, while we enjoy and are blessed by the observance of the sacrament He gave us. Therefore He guides the pen of the Apostle so that he writes to remind us that, "As often as ye eat this bread, and drink the cup, ye proclaim the Lord's death *till he come.*" Backward, to the days of the lesser light, the days of the older time, the feast of the mere memorial and type; and forward to the days of the greater light, the days of His visible appearing, the time when death shall be swallowed up in victory, are we bidden to look when partaking of the feast of His presence,— a feast so much richer than the former, so inferior to the latter feast of new wine, in His Kingdom.

The Passover was celebrated on the eve of a great deliverance; the Lord's Supper, on the eve of a far greater deliverance; that future feast shall be in memory of a full deliverance. The Passover was first eaten under the shadow of a perilous undertaking; the Lord's Supper, in the shadow of Gethsemane and Calvary; that coming supper will have no shadows. The Passover was eaten by a million people, bound together by a common need and a common hope; the Lord's Supper was eaten by a dozen men, bound together in the communion of One

Lord and one love; the coming feast shall be partaken of by the millions upon millions of redeemed from every tribe and nation and kindred and people, bound together by the common experience of grace in their deliverance, and by the blessed tie of the One Fatherhood and their one brotherhood. Three wonderful feasts,— Egypt—Palestine—Heaven!

Thirsty soul, dost thou not long for that coming feast? We shall not need to feed upon Him then, since need for the remission of sins will be past—no more sin. The need for sensible manifestations of His presence will be gone—no more doubt. The need for remembrance will be superseded—no more parting. We shall sit down beside Him, you and I, in communion most intimate and precious, at the time of that new Lord's Supper.

1. An exhibition of *divine unselfish love* is found in the establishment of this Holy Supper. Think of the sorrows upon Him and before Him: Gethsemane, the treachery of Judas, the arrest, the abandonment by His disciples. At such a time as this, He could think of His children; of the need for some central mark and ceremony of fellowship; of the comfort and help this would give them in the later history of the Church; of this means of perpetuating His real presence among them, in a way that

should strengthen the faith and quicken the life of those who should come to Him. Wonderful love—unselfish love—the love that breathes through all His life, and especially through those last addresses and prayers.

2. It is a manifestation of *divine power*. None but God could institute, for all time, such a mystery, a strangely simple, sacred, peculiar feast, "in remembrance" of Him, imparting, as He said, "my body," "the new covenant in my blood." How well He knew the fate before Him, whose creeping, deepening shadow the dull disciples had not yet discerned! How well He understood what we can never comprehend, namely, His sacramental presence at every time and place where the Holy Supper is celebrated, to feed us and strengthen us with His body and blood, given for us.

3. We ought to *appreciate and use the feast*. Instituted so solemnly; evidencing so tenderly the Saviour's love; serving as His last will and testament; giving us an opportunity to show His death and point to His coming again,—we ought not to think lightly of feasting here, or to count it a little thing. It meets our need for individual assurance. It goes beyond the written Word in that it gives me a participation in the slain body and the outpoured blood, which are mine as surely as the bit of bread and the sip of wine are mine. The Holy

Sacrament singles out each one who partakes of it, and gives to each, alone, the assurance that He receives, in pledge and seal of His salvation, the very sacrifice of Calvary. Can you neglect and despise such heavenly food of grace as this? Is it enough, when He spreads this table furnished so rarely, to pass it by, to come but seldom? Oh, shall we not by frequent communion with Him thus, be better fitted to enjoy the new wine in the Father's kingdom, where He who kept the best wine till the last, shall be our Host? Oh, come in, Heavenly Guest! Let me feed on Thee, Heavenly Bread! Let me drink of Thee, Wine of eternal Life! And Thine shall be the praise and glory evermore.

Prayer. O Saviour, Who hast provided at such cost this sacred feast, give me hunger and thirst for that refreshment which it offers me. Fit me for a worthy reception of Thyself. Robe me in the wedding garment, that I may not dishonor Thee, nor have Thy condemnation. Make me strong through the food Thou givest, and let me go, in the strength of this meat, faithfully to do Thy will. As I receive Thee, take me into the secret place of Thy rest and love, and give me precious communion. Keep Thou a place for me at the feast where Thou shalt drink again of the fruit of the vine, and let me sit with Thee there! Hasten the day to which Thou dost point us as often as we come to the Holy Supper, the day when Thou shalt return, and when we shall be forever with the Lord. *Amen.*

Good Friday

The Jews therefore, because it was the Preparation, that the bodies should not remain on the cross upon the sabbath (for the day of that sabbath was a high *day*), asked of Pilate that their legs might be broken, and *that* they might be taken away. The soldiers therefore came, and brake the legs of the first, and of the other who was crucified with him: but when they came to Jesus, and saw that he was dead already, they brake not his legs: howbeit one of the soldiers with a spear pierced his side, and straightway there came out blood and water. And he that hath seen hath borne witness, and his witness is true: and he knoweth that he saith true, that ye also may believe. For these things came to pass, that the scripture might be fulfilled, A bone of him shall not be broken. And again another scripture saith, They shall look on him whom they pierced.

And when even was now come, because it was the Preparation, that is, the day before the sabbath, there came a rich man, Joseph of Arimathea, a councillor of honorable estate, who also himself was Jesus' disciple, but secretly, for fear of the Jews, and was looking for the kingdom of God; he had not consented unto their counsel and deed; and he boldly went in unto Pilate, and asked for the body of Jesus. And Pilate marvelled if he were already dead: and calling unto him the centurion, he asked him whether he had been any while dead. And when he learned it of the centurion, he granted the corpse to Joseph.

And there came also Nicodemus, he who at the first came to him by night, bringing a mixture of myrrh and aloes, about a hundred pound *weight*. So they took the body of Jesus, and bound it in linen cloths with the spices, as the custom of the Jews is to bury. Now in the place where he was crucified there was a garden; and in the garden his own new tomb, which had been hewn out of a rock, wherein was never man yet laid. There then because of the Jews' Preparation (for the tomb was nigh at hand) they laid Jesus, and rolled a great stone to the door of the tomb and departed.

And the women, that had come with him out of Galilee, followed after, and beheld the tomb, and how his body was laid. And they returned, and prepared spices and ointments.

And on the sabbath they rested according to the commandment.

Prophecies Fulfilled. Again the tender consciences of the Jews are troubled; this time, by the prospect of the defilement of their approaching holy day, from the presence of the dead bodies on the cross. As it is not to be supposed that the crucified will die for hours to come, Pilate is entreated to order the soldiers to hasten their death, by the brutal method of breaking their legs. They begin the task, and are amazed, when they come to Jesus, to find Him already dead! But they must make sure, so one of them thrusts his spear into the side of Jesus, and the blood and water stream forth. He who saw it, bore testimony, and remembered how it was written: "Not a bone of Him shall be broken;" and again, "They shall look on Him whom they have pierced." But there was another prophecy, quite at variance, apparently, with all that has gone before, which must now come to fulfilment.

"They made His grave with the rich in His death." (Isa. 53: 9.) How could it be possible for a criminal, executed by crucifixion, to lie in a rich man's grave? God's Word is sure, and will not fail. There was a certain rich man, a member of the Sanhedrin, but one who had not consented to their evil deed. Before Jesus died the shameful death of a malefactor, He had been afraid to confess Himself a disciple. But now, when those who had been known as His disciples forsook and denied Him, this man became bold, and resolved, at any risk, to pay the last honors to the body of his Lord. Dearer than all his wealth, he values, now, the dead body of the Master. He is brave enough to go to Pilate and ask for the treasure, which is granted him. There is another at the burial, a secret disciple like Joseph; Nicodemus, to whom, in that night interview, the Lord had spoken the wonderful words about the new birth. He also was led of the Spirit in this hour of seeming disaster, to come out on the side of Christ, and be numbered with the faithful few. They wrapped the beloved body in linen cloths, with spices for embalming, and bore the burden tenderly to the new rock-hewn sepulchre of Joseph, in the near-by garden. The women were with them. The burial must be hurried, as the day of Preparation for the Passover was at hand. They laid Him in the little vault, and it is noted, especially of the women, that " they beheld the tomb, and how His body was laid." This is related because it became of interest on the Easter morning. The story is very brief and simple. What heavy hearts were in the breasts of those who composed the little funeral train; what tears were shed; what words were spoken; what crushed hopes and bitter disappointment filled them, we are not told. They turned away. Honored, at least by the few, in His death; sleeping not in an accursed tomb, but in a rich man's sepulchre; wrapped in that still slumber from which they little thought He was so soon to wake, they leave Him. And the loving women, eager to do still more for Him, go back and prepare the spices and ointments for His complete embalmment when the Sabbath shall be past.

1. *To wait until our friends are dead*, to honor them, is not good; yet it is often done. Too frequent are the stories of men of genius who starve, body and heart, to be afterward applauded and honored with every token of enthusiastic appreciation. We cannot but think how the love of Joseph and Nicodemus would have cheered the heart of Jesus when He was doing His work, and how much their influence might have wrought for other lives. But they waited.

They were not cowards. Probably they had not expected to delay until His ears could not hear their words of trust and affection, and they could only offer Him the hospitality of a tomb and the honor of a respectful burial. They had lost opportunities that could not come again. Thus is it with many, even now. They trust Him, and they are, in their secret hearts, His children; but they wait. They delay the giving of their service. They expect, some day, to honor Him with rich benefactions. They will confess Him when their "convenient season" shall have come. Beware lest you wait too long!

2. There is *something noble in this espousal of a cause that was at its lowest ebb.* There was something noble in the courage which confessed Him when so few were to be found who would reverence His Name, and when worship might mean danger. However they had erred in the past, we are sure these men will never flinch in the future. There was true manhood in their allegiance to the dead Christ, though they had failed in duty to Him, living. Even if their confession meant nothing more than personal love and admiration for Him, based on what He had said and done; even if they had no trust in Him such as He deserves, still it was brave and manly. So He needs hearts of oak to confess Him now. He needs men and women

not afraid nor ashamed to stand for Him and face His foes. God give us men to acknowledge Christ, to love Him, to serve Him, to endure hardships as good soldiers of this Captain. Are you of these? Can you have followed Him in all these steps of His path of love unto death, and now desert Him or deny Him, or fail to confess Him valorously? God forbid!

3. *The rich, too, have a right to Jesus.* Not many mighty, not many noble, after the flesh, but *some*, thank God, do follow Him. And He welcomes them. There is a place for riches in His service. Only consecrate wealth, with all else, to Jesus, and He can sanctify and use it. A great privilege was this of the rich man, that he could do for the Lord's body what others, who loved Him as well, could not do. So is it a privilege to-day, to send forth missionaries, to found Christian schools and homes of mercy, to sustain and extend the work of the Church, out of the possessions He has given you. Oh, what a day that will be, when men and women who are able, shall have learned the joy of lavishing their abundance unstintedly on the Lord who bought them. What is your Lenten offering of gratitude to Him to-day? Ask yourself, and let your love dictate the answer. Love asks not, "With how little giving can I escape?" but, "How much is it possible for me to give?" What is your gift? He

does not need a tomb now, but can you not build Him a temple?

Prayer. O Lord, I thank Thee that, lifted up, Thou art already drawing men to Thee. My heart goes out to the rich man who would not let Thee lie in a pauper's grave. I rejoice that Thou hast a place for every offering. If I cannot give Thee a splendid sepulchre, I can bring Thee spices. What is mine, O Lord, is Thine! Take it, and bless and use it. Make me ever brave and true and faithful, that more than all other gifts to Thee, my life may always praise Thee. *Amen.*

Saturday after Palmarum

Now on the morrow, which is *the day* after the Preparation, the chief priests and the Pharisees were gathered together unto Pilate, saying, Sir, we remember that that deceiver said, while he was yet alive, After three days I rise again. Command therefore that the sepulchre be made sure until the third day, lest haply his disciples come and steal him away, and say unto the people, He is risen from the dead: and the last error will be worse than the first. Pilate said unto them, Ye have a guard: go, make it as sure as ye can. So they went, and made the sepulchre sure, sealing the stone, the guard being with them.

The Master sleeps. The long hours pass slowly while He lies upon His stony couch. His soul is in the Paradise where on this day after the crucifixion, the repentant thief is with Him, in His bliss. His body has not yet been quickened, that in His completeness He may descend into the hell of Satan and lost spirits, to triumph there. This day is a day of silence and of rest. Let the poor, torn body lie there, its time of toil and trial all passed by. The friends who loved Him, but who do not know of the glorious triumph yet before Him, must be glad that His head is pillowed now on the bosom of death, instead of on the shameful cross; that the chill of the last sleep is on Him, and not the fever of those last hours of life. One would think there must be joy in hell, to-day, that the Conqueror is conquered, and the Life-giver dead. And deep must be the satisfaction of His high-priestly enemies, that the grave holds Him, and He is out of their way, to thwart and disturb them no longer. But they are not yet satisfied. A peace-destroying recollection comes over them. He had often said a strange thing which they now remembered. They had perverted the statement when they told how He had said: "Destroy this temple, and in three days I will build it up." They know He meant the temple of His body; and a deadly fear comes over them. So many of His wonderful words had come true, what if it should be made to appear that this also was fulfilled? Then all they had accomplished might be worse than useless. Perhaps the disciples may come, and, stealing away the body, proclaim Him risen. Then the last error would be worse than the first. They must appeal again to Pilate, they must secure the aid of the imperial government to prevent the miscarriage of their aims. Let but the seal of Rome be put upon the closed sepulchre, with a Roman guard at the door, and all may yet be safe. No sooner planned than done! The priests and Pharisees, unable to rest even while He sleeps in the tomb, gather and tell their story to the governor. He grants their request. A Roman guard of sixty soldiers, invincible, not knowing fear, go to the grave. Across the stone they place a cord, fastening it on either side with a lump of wax on which is stamped the seal of the Cæsars. The sepulchre is sure. Now His enemies can rest. Their last apprehension is removed.—But all they have done is nothing. The dispirited, despairing disciples have no leader, no plan, nor any hope. Safeguard surer than all, they have even forgotten the word of the Master which His enemies remembered. And in the dignity of death, in the darkness of the rocky cave, the Master sleeps on, undisturbed by the jesting and the oaths and the tramping of the guard outside. The prisoner of the Roman soldiers; the prisoner of Death. Let Him rest in peace till the time for awaking comes!

1. This day should be to us *a day of stillness*. Let the soul be quiet, pondering deeply on this great mystery, recalling the way of the cross and the meaning of these strange events. A day for prayer; a day for rest in God, for intimate communion with self and with the Saviour. Let the day's accustomed tasks be set aside while reverently we enter into the secret place beneath the shadow of His wing. Noise, restlessness, busy hurrying, and care are not befitting. Let us enjoy the Sabbath of the soul. "In quietness and confidence shall be

your strength." (Is. 30: 15.) It is the time to wait for God. "Be still and know that I am God." And while you wait *for* Him, wait *upon* Him, and "Renew your strength!" (Ps. 62: 1, 5.)

2. *A true word from false foes* was that wherein they said that if He rose from the dead "the last error would be worse than the first." For Him to yield, without the least resistance, to the tomb and all His foes, then to triumph over all,—this was greater proof of His Messianic claims than if He had resisted, and prevented the working of those evil wills upon Him. Weak were the Roman soldiers when the angel of the resurrection stood before them, and the earth quaked beneath them. Little counted the seal of Rome's Emperor, when the ambassador of the King of Kings rolled the stone away. Helpless was Satan, and amazed, when He saw the Saviour, in that body which the Prince of Hell had done to death, stand before Him in his own domain and tell his triumph! And to this day the victory over death and the grave is the strength of the Gospel message.

3. Sore loss is always theirs who *forget the Word of God*. Jesus had again and again prepared His disciples for His death, and for His victory over death, yet they had forgotten. Peace, instead of horrible despair, would have

been their portion all through the awful scenes that they had witnessed, if they had but received and remembered His Word. With the quietness and confidence that would have been their strength, they could have waited for Him while He slept if they had but remembered His repeated promise: "After three days I shall rise again." His enemies remembered, yet He had not spoken for them; His friends, whom His words were to comfort, forgot. We, too, lose so much of peace, when trial and loss beset us, because we have forgotten the words He gave to strengthen us in just such hours. In His blessed Book there is that which we need for every circumstance of life. Let us "eat the roll," and it will be "sweet within us!"

Prayer. O Christ, though Thou liest in the tomb, Thou art yet the Prince of Life. Out of Thy blood comes blessing to Thy children. Out of Thy death comes life to those who trust. Out of Thy tomb comes victory, for Thou hast robbed death and sin and hell of all their power to terrify Thine own. We do not fear, because we know that naught can hold Thee. On this day of stillness, calm Thou our hearts and give us trust, while we watch to see Thee rise in Thine unwearied might. Give us to know the power of Thy resurrection. Help us to live in Thee. Spread Thou a tabernacle over us through all our journey. By Thy pilgrimage from Gethsemane to Golgotha, make Thou our way secure from earth to Heaven; since we ask it all through Thee our Mediator, Who with the Father and the Holy Ghost, livest and reignest ever one God, world without end, *Amen.*

www.ingramcontent.com/pod-product-compliance
Lightning Source LLC
Chambersburg PA
CBHW022015220426
43663CB00007B/1084